WORKING RELATIONSHIPS

*Crisis and resilience at the heart
of employee experience*

Aaron Delgaty

Praise for **WORKING RELATIONSHIPS**

"'Working Relationships' is a brilliant dive into the world of work that truly unlocks how and why our relationship with work can change our lives for better or worse. Through storytelling and practical guidance, Delgaty explores the concepts of continuity, reciprocity, purpose, and hope in a workplace still reeling from the whiplash of changes experienced over the past four years. If you've ever wondered why you've felt disengaged for no reason, had struggling coworkers wonder how they can make a difference, or led a team that can't seem to put the pieces together to perform under pressure, this book is for you. Most importantly, it has clear answers to help navigate the journey to a healthier perspective and approach to work as a whole."

—Lance Haun, Vice President, Market Insights, The Starr Conspiracy

"Dr. Aaron Delgaty takes a data-backed deep dive into the core Employee Experience challenge of the 2020s workplace — the burnout and lack of purpose so many employees are feeling today. Most importantly, he doesn't just diagnose the problem; he offers hope and clear direction for work leaders trying to improve the resilience of their people and their organizations today. Highly recommended."

—Steve Smith, Partner, The Starr Conspiracy

"In 'Working Relationships,' Aaron Delgaty masterfully illustrates the intricate tapestry of human connection that underlies the professional realm. This book serves as a lighthouse, guiding through the tumultuous seas of organizational change with the resilient threads of continuity, reciprocity, purpose, and hope. It's a manifesto for those who believe in the transformative power of work as a relational and meaningful pursuit."

— Dr. Keith Keating, BDO Chief Learning Officer, author of The Trusted Learning Advisor: The Tools, Techniques and Skills You Need to Make L&D a Business Priority.

"In 'Working Relationships: Crisis and Resilience at the Heart of Employee Experience,' Aaron Delgaty delivers an indispensable resource for learning and development professionals seeking to elevate workplace dynamics and employee engagement. Aaron's nuanced exploration of continuity, reciprocity, purpose, and hope sheds light on the foundational elements that underpin successful organizational learning cultures. This book is a clarion call to those committed to fostering environments where development and growth are not just encouraged but also are integral to the fabric of the organization. His insights are both a reflection of his deep understanding of the workplace and a practical guide for professionals aiming to unlock the full potential of their teams. An essential read for learning and development practitioners dedicated to crafting resilient, thriving workspaces."

— *Sean Stowers - CEO, Chief Learning Officer, WeLearn*

Aaron Delgaty
Working Relationships
Crisis and resilience at the heart of employee experience
The Starr Conspiracy Publishing
Fort Worth, TX
© 2024, Aaron Delgaty

For Lauren & Elsie
An artisan's heart flourishes in the comfort of a loving home.

Acknowledgments

This book, like the work it explores, was made possible by myriad relationships. I'm happy and proud to say that the cast of those who have given their time, wisdom, and encouragement has only grown since I submitted the first version of this book as my dissertation project in 2020.

My deepest gratitude to Chris Nelson, my dissertation advisor, whose invitation to the University of North Carolina at Chapel Hill launched this project, and whose support, patience, insight, and interest as a mentor have left an indelible mark on me as an anthropologist and artisan. My sincere appreciation to my committee members, Margaret Wiener, Peter Redfield, Townsend Middleton, and Brad Weiss, for generously lending your expertise, for helping smooth the rough edges and fill the gaps of this work, and for seeing promise when I could not. Thank you to the professors, fellow graduate students, and support staff of UNC's Anthropology Department: Rudi Colloredo-Mansfeld, Jocelyn Chua, Paul Leslie, Gabby Purcell, Katie Barrett, Chu-Wen Hsieh, Paul Schissel, Sora Enomoto, Dayuma Alban, Bryan Dougan, Eric Thomas, Katie Poor, and Irina Olenicheva. I could not have asked for a warmer community or greater friends. Thank you as well to my professors and colleagues from the University of Texas at Austin: Robert Oppenheim, John Traphagan, Heather Hindman, Ben Miller, and Erin Newton. While not directly involved in this project, our time together helped establish the intellectual and methodological foundation on which this book is built.

This project would not have been possible without the generosity of the artisans, business owners, people leaders, and other professionals whose stories and experiences helped fill the pages of this book. A special thanks to the artisans who taught me first to brew, distill, and craft cheese while putting up with my peculiar questions and itinerant lifestyle. Thank you to the many farmers, distributors, businesses owners, bartenders, customers, and other people connectors who at various times created connections and shared their insights. Thank you as well to the reviewers and staff of the Japan Foundation for funding and facilitating the dissertation research that forms the cornerstone of this project.

My heartfelt appreciation to those who helped me pivot to industry research and strategy—Lance Haun, Jonathan Goodman, and Steve Smith—mentors who helped me find my sea legs in unfamiliar waters and in doing so breathed new life into this project. Thank you to Rachit Malhotra, Steve Smith, Ashley Bernard, Kristin Berry, Lou Chapman, Joanna Castle, Ashley Dillon, Erin Sanders, Racheal Bates, Nancy Crabb, Erin Swan, Kevin Mangum, Matt Tatum, Erin Magee, and Jeff Peterson for creating a professional community where I could explore bold ideas. My immense gratitude and love to Sean Stowers and Loren Sanders, friends, colleagues, and confidants whose collaboration and friendship is the spice of life, professional and otherwise.

Thank you to Lance Haun, Jonathan Goodman, Ashley Bernard, and Rachit Malhotra for reading early versions of this manuscript and graciously offering the edits, insights, and questions that added additional breadth, depth, and clarity to the finished book. Thank you Bret Starr for furnishing the talent, experience, and resources to make this book a reality. And thank you to Dana Karpinski for your persistent kindness, and for making all of the trains run on time. My deepest appreciation to Kenny Porter, my best friend and fellow writer, for being a model of resilience. Laughing and commiserating with you has been an unfailing source of strength.

While so many have supported me throughout this adventure, only one has been my partner. Lauren, your fearless optimism has seen me through this journey's many storms. Thank you for always reminding me of who I am, where I've been, and where I'm going. You are the best part of me.

And finally, to Elsie, my brave, precocious, beautiful little girl. From the first time I saw you, the first time I held you, from your first smile, your first tantrum, for every giggle and tiny handhold, and for all the nights spent dozing on my chest while I wrote this, you have been— and continue every day to be—my inspiration. You are my heart.

What's to Come

Preface

THE EVERYDAY CRISIS OF WORK

One of the most important realizations I've had in the interim between finishing the dissertation in 2020 that would become the pilot for this book and writing this manuscript is how beside the point the experiences that became the focus of my dissertation research proved to be. It's not that what I studied during my doctorate wasn't important—I still think crisis was and continues to be important to understanding the nature of human relationships to work. Rather, it's that when I gave myself the necessary time and distance to view my original thesis, and especially through the lens of the subsequent pandemic and economic uncertainty that followed graduation, I realized the presence or absence of crisis in relation to work wasn't the big story, the wicked problem, or whatever professional idiom you want to use for the thing at the heart of the matter.

I subtitled my dissertation "Fermentation in a Time of Crisis," my idea being to highlight the practical, social, and philosophical realities of working in and through moments of sustained personal or social upheaval. Now having settled down from itinerant research to work as a professional researcher, putting down personal and professional roots, I've realized that work is never really removed from crisis. **Work needs crisis**. It's the impetus for us to get to work. To say one works in times of crisis is like saying that one speculates in times of uncertainty. That's kind of the whole point. The situation—crisis, uncertainty, etc.—creates the need for action.

Crisis is also the ever-present backdrop of the stage on which our work takes place. Our world is constantly in motion, people and things and forces moving and interacting in ways that are often unexpected, sometimes upsetting, and always partially outside of our control. This generates a constant stream of crises. Whether it be macroeconomic downturns caused by wars or a global pandemic, or an office funk caused by a broken coffee maker or someone's cat passing away, there is always some configuration of fresh and stale crises at hand that colors the context of our working lives. (This is what makes workplace optimization such a soul-crushing endeavor—it's never perfect, and it's never going to be.) It's crisis as usual.

But the commonality of crisis is exactly what makes it so meaningful to the world of work, and so important to study as the context to the work we do. Anthropologists have a habit of saying that things go without saying because they come without saying. The objective of research—or at least anthropological research on human culture—is to disrupt that flow in an attempt to understand why the things that go *do* go, and why that *going* has become so unremarkable. We are so used to thinking of work as "just work" that until we step back and look at what we do abstractly, we don't realize that our working lives are really just the everyday management of crises of varying magnitudes: to address a customer's need, to put out a boardroom fire, to fix a broken machine, to pay the bills, to ease boredom. In the Work Tech space, it seems like everyone refers to their products as "solutions," solutions to the crises of weak employee engagement or broken talent pipelines. We work to make our worlds a little less chaotic. And when the work we do creates additional problems, we do more work to solve those too—we accidentally or intentionally make our lives a little more chaotic, and then create the solution to that chaos. (The proliferation of cordless phones leads to a crisis of how to charge them, protect them, and find them between the couch cushions.) It's kind of absurd, but it's also fine. It's *human*. Without crisis, work wouldn't have a point.

Naturally, this realization left me with another crisis: If crisis were the point of work and always in the background of work, then maybe the presence of crisis itself wasn't why some businesses and professionals would fail. Was there something more fundamental to our experience of work that had a direct impact on whether we as individuals, teams, and organizations would succeed or fail? Was there something that could give insight into not only how we work, but *why* we get out of bed in the first place? Was there something unmistakably *human* at the heart of our work that could serve as a litmus test for not only whether the endeavor would be successful, but more important, worthwhile? I think so. I think it's relationships.

Humans are fundamentally social creatures. We can't help but create and become deeply invested in relationships. When we work, humans generate not only solutions and crises and solutions to those crises, but also connections: connections between ourselves and the work we do, ourselves and the people with whom we work, and ourselves and the institutions for whom we work. These relationships interest us, entertain us, sustain us, and inspire us. When they become toxic, they can also hurt us, vex us, degrade us, disillusion us, and even kill us. These relationships are the point—they are how we play, why we play, and what we play for.

This book is about how our working relationships come to be and the different elements—continuity, reciprocity, purpose, and hope—that shape our relationships. In the following pages, I consider why working relationships matter, the personal and organizational circumstances that can strengthen these relationships, and the pressures and pains that can cause them to snap. This book is also about the meaning of working relationships, not just to me as an anthropologist and researcher, but to you as a fellow human, someone who lives and works within a tangled bank of interpersonal connections. This book is about starting a dialogue with yourself about what those relationships look like for you, and what they could and should look like.

Introduction

RELATIONSHIPS ALL THE WAY DOWN

Work is all about relationships. I wanted to build to that point at the end of this chapter, but a colleague told me I should stop grandstanding like a stage magician and just get to the "ta-da." Work is fundamentally relationship-driven—pushed, pulled, lifted, or sunk by the connections between people and the work they do, the people with whom they work, and the institutions for which they work. These working relationships are woven from four elemental threads: **continuity, reciprocity, purpose**, and **hope**. These elements are intertwined and mutually influencing. When they are present in great enough concentration and quality, our experience of work tends to go well. We tend to be well. And the communities, organizations, and institutions that our work sustains—and that sustain our work—tend to flourish. When these relationships are neglected, the quality and sustainability of our work and work experience dips. When continuity, reciprocity, purpose, and hope are absent, everything collapses.

I came to this observation by way of a brewery, although it would take me over a decade before I realized the significance of the experience. At the time, I was just hot, bored, and a little drunk.

In 2012, I traveled to the coast of Japan's northeastern Tōhoku region to survey the local recovery efforts following the 2011 earthquake, tsunami, and nuclear meltdown. I was in Iwate Prefecture, which had been hit pretty hard and was close enough to Fukushima that local governments had launched public announcement campaigns assuring residents and visitors that the produce was safe. I was working with a small Zen Buddhist temple, about 100 km inland from the Pacific Ocean, observing and assisting in the funeral rituals that the two priests—an elderly man and thirty-something son-in-law—carried out for its increasingly gray community. I had come to Tōhoku to study the aftermath of the triple disaster but found a much slower burning, if related, crisis: the gradual depopulation of rural Japan, and the quiet struggle of rural institutions like community temples and local public health centers to mitigate the social and emotional fallout of empty houses and broken families. But the temple I worked with was in a network of Zen temples that stretched all over the prefecture, including the battered coast. By way of assisting at these affiliate temples, I found myself at a sake brewery in Miyako.

It was a muggy July day on the bus into Miyako City. I was part of a tour group of mostly elderly pensioners bound for a memorial service farther up the coast for the victims of the 2011 earthquake and tsunami. The head priest of my temple was filling in for a colleague and would be traveling in the back seat of a deacon's sedan, but I opted to ride ahead with the community members to see more of the event (and to avoid the deacon's chain-smoking). Despite the solemnity of our purpose, the tour group scheduled time ahead of the memorial service to observe the ravaged coastline. This form of dark tourism had become increasingly common in the past year, popping up even before the aftershocks settled. We went to Miyako's port district. The seaside was a vacant expanse of overgrown foundations interrupted only by an impromptu general store in a trailer and a handful of shacks and camping tents erected by residents who refused to abandon their property. Among the skeletal remains of former residences and businesses was a sake brewery, a lone brick warehouse left standing following the wave. A desiccated brown sakabayashi (a bundle of cedar needles) hung above the main entrance announcing the end of the brewing cycle. This month was the brewery's first run since the disaster.

Standing within the brewhouse, the owners—a middle-aged couple—pointed out the scars of the past year's trauma: discolored bricks marking the flood line, a snaking crack through a supporting wall, a 15-foot stainless steel fermentation vessel lying in a crumpled heap in the far corner where the wave left it. The owners stood next to a pallet of freshly packed boxes, handing out samples and selling bottles to the tour group. The spirit tasted like sake, nothing particularly remarkable. But perhaps that's what was remarkable about it. Despite all the tragedy, the human cost, the upheaval of the landscape and everyday life, people could still make sake that tasted like sake. To those tasting the unblemished spirit, the brewery stood as an icon of local resilience. "Yoku ganbarimashita," one gruff elderly man told the owners, "You did well."

That unexpected trip to a brewery ultimately proved to be a crossroads in my research and in my worldview. Initially, I was a little riled by the whole thing. Popping by a brewery on the way to a mass wake seemed somewhat inappropriate, and the brewery owners came off as more than a bit ghoulish. There would have been a really low-hanging article to write about disaster opportunism. However, when I stopped being such a prude and started thinking about the broader context in which the transaction took place, the brewery visit took on a different meaning. For the owners, I imagine the bottles arranged on the shipping floor and the money exchanging hands served as tangible indicators of personal recovery. The continuity of brewing again. The reciprocity of serving a community. The purpose of industry. The hope that the brewery, its operators, and its customers, though still bound to the disaster through memories and scars that would only partially fade, were nevertheless moving forward. Moving forward together.

Reframed, I think this brewery experience—my first ever in a career that would unexpectedly be full of them—ultimately piqued the curiosity that would, years down the line, coalesce into this book. Relationships. As I share in the chapter on hope, the point of a funeral isn't really the deceased. They're dead, and what happens to them after death is guesswork. The practicality of a funeral is bringing the community together in the aftermath of a loss to remind them that their family, friends, and neighbors are still here. Their relationships, though changed by crisis, are still intact. Although I wouldn't be able to realize this connection until I had settled down and invested in a personal and professional community of my own, that's what the brewery visit was all about. It wasn't a sales ploy. It was a reminder of who remained and what kept them tied together.

This book is about this belated revelation, one that led to a whole flurry of questions: What is the connection between the work we do, the communities in which we live and serve, and the crises that we navigate alone and together? In the chaotic world of work, why do some succeed and some fail? Is there a fundamental substance that forms the bedrock of our working lives and, if so, how can we test the resilience of this foundation before it is too late? I already gave it away at the beginning of this chapter, but it's about relationships. Like turtles endlessly stacked on top of turtles to support the world, *our experience of work is relationships all the way down*. When these relationships are stable and rewarding, we—and the communities in and for which we live and work—are resilient. When these relationships fail, so do we all.

In the following pages, I unravel working relationships and the elemental threads of continuity, reciprocity, purpose, and hope that sustain them. I consider the following:

1. What creates working relationships?

2. What makes our working relationships resilient?

3. How can we better understand the idiosyncratic motivators and demotivators of our own working relationships?

Before I get into all of that, though, I'd like to talk about how I got here.

4

A wandering apprenticeship

I owe a great debt to my advisor, Chris Nelson, for his suggestion to temper theory with a healthy dose of practical experience. It was 2015 and I was writing my dissertation research prospectus, having shifted focus from the 2011 Tōhoku disaster to the slower-burning crises of economic and social precariousness, and from the quiet contemplation of the temple to the hectic industry of artisanal alcohol production. Chris recommended I step outside the library and see if any members of the Research Triangle's burgeoning craft breweries or distilleries would be willing to let me shadow them for a production day. Maybe hands-on practice, immersed in the sights and sounds and heat, would illuminate some concept or question that remained obscure in the confines of a university office.

Once in the field, I became a sort of wandering apprentice, a term I borrow from Anthony Bourdain, who described the process of chefs bouncing from restaurant to restaurant to collect new ideas and hone their skills before settling down in their own establishment.[1] Greg Downey argues that apprenticeship serves as a valuable means not only to learn new skills, but also to learn how practitioners learn.[2] I became an itinerant artisan-in-training, drifting from North Carolina's Research Triangle to Tokyo, to Okinawa, and back to Carolina in search of new working practices, environments, and philosophies. At times, I was taken on as an actual apprentice, a formal relationship (read: ass-kicking) directly under a journeyman or master artisan. Most times, however, I was engaged in what Mary Nagata calls an informal apprenticeship: a working environment in which on-the-job training is the typical and preferred (sometimes only) method of instruction.[3]

Surprisingly (to me at least), finding places to apprentice turned

---

[1] See Anthony Bourdain's Kitchen Confidential (2007:256).

[2] See Greg Downey's Learning capoeira: Lessons in cunning from an Afro-Brazilian art (2005:53).

[3] Nagata 2007:36

out to be one of the easier aspects of my project. At the time I conducted research, brewing was in a rapid growth phase (industry publications and even popular business outlets like *Forbes* were regularly posting stories on the explosive growth in the number of craft breweries across the country). Brewery owners were looking to expand as rapidly as they could on as tight a budget as possible. Like family restaurants or family farms, spouses, children, neighbors, extended relatives, and friends were often pressured into helping out with bartending, canning, running festivals, or whatever easy-to-do position needed a warm body (and not much else). In a context of floating volunteer help, I was a pretty good find because (1) I cost the same as their other volunteers (i.e., nothing), (2) I typically hung around longer than their relatives and friends who became tired or bored after a day or week of pouring beers or standing in a tent handing out samples, and (3) in the event that they became sick of me, they could politely (or brusquely) tell me to fuck off without burning any bridges.

Interestingly, the days of easy and open volunteering largely dried up by the time I transitioned to a professional brewer in 2018. Craft brewing was still very popular, and there were a lot of bored professionals and recent high-school and college graduates looking for something to do that didn't involve a suit and tie, combat fatigues, or a production line. However, the market had started to contract and breweries had matured professionally to the point that they realized that letting people drift in and out while representing the business wasn't safe, efficient, or a fun experience for the permanent staff. "Imagine," one brewer told me, "that every fucking day is Willy Wonka's chocolate factory. We're the Oompa Loompas, and we can't get anything done because these assholes keep falling in the chocolate." That pretty much summed up why the West stopped being so wild.

I was fortunate in that I got in—and out—at the right moment. In all except one instance—when an assistant Buddhist priest threw me out of his temple (I share this story later)—I initiated the departure. I typically hung around for as long as I felt was necessary to get a good feel for the everyday rhythms and interpersonal dynamics of a place. I watched an anime once that claimed you could get to really understand a place in three days. That's bullshit. Three months was more reasonable, but a year—a full four-season cycle—was typically ideal. I would leave when I felt there was nothing much left to learn, when eight-hour shifts started giving diminishing returns, or when something in my personal or academic life made it inconvenient to stay. On a couple of occasions, the apprenticeship morphed into something more like actual employment, with management scheduling me to work regular hours and to work alone. The former was appreciated because it gave me some consistency. The latter was not, because it meant I had no one to talk to, to learn from, or to observe. I exited those situations fairly quickly.

The wandering apprenticeship approach to research had its advantages. For one, regularly switching locations and sometimes industries provided a diverse image of the techniques, perspectives, and environments that made up the world of work I studied. I had a lot of different kinds of paint, and I was able to paint with a broad brush. Multi-sited studies, the academic term for bouncing around, lend themselves to comparison. While you don't gain the deep insight into everyday culture that someone who spends five years in a single village does, you do pick up on cross-cultural patterns. In my case, I noticed commonalities in how, where, and why people worked across radically different industrial, social, economic, and cultural contexts. I focus on working relationships and the fundamental elements of those relationships—continuity, reciprocity, purpose, and hope—because those are the things that kept popping up over and over again whether I was in a Japanese temple or an American brewery. Humans are very different, and also very much the same.

My approach to research wasn't all upside, though. My persistent lack of permanency was also a drawback in terms of my becoming a community insider. Can you really call yourself a brewer, a priest, a teacher, or any sort of *real* professional if you aren't committed to the profession? A lot of my colleagues would have said "no." As a result, in my apprenticeship days, I was often treated more as an outsider or interloper, closer to the family and friend volunteers than an actual part of the team. As one brewer friend put it, I didn't really have any "skin in the game"; it didn't really matter if I succeeded or failed as a brewer, because it wouldn't impact my career as an academic or researcher. I would be able to teach my class or write my book regardless of what happened. Not being paid was really convenient for ownership in terms of free labor, but it also meant that they—and by extension those who directly managed me—didn't have leverage. I could bounce at any time.

I didn't appreciate this point until I was a head brewer myself and had my first volunteer apprenticeship. It was precisely at the moment when, three hours late into a canning day (an absolute shit show under the best of circumstances), my coworker—attached to the brewery as part of an apprenticeship program for retired service people—rolled in with a coffee and wearing an aloha shirt and flip-flops. Mind-blowing for me, but a non-event for him. What did it matter? He wasn't being paid, so I wasn't really his boss. He was also working on starting his own brewery with a GI grant, so he didn't really need this job anyway. (And it wasn't really a job, again, because he wasn't getting paid.) In other words, we weren't in a true working relationship as I would come to understand that concept later and as I explore in this book.

Job-hopping and working outside the conditions of traditional employment (i.e., not getting paid) meant I didn't have to commit to any one situation. However, it also meant I wasn't investing the necessary time, energy, and commitment to develop relationships with my coworkers, the business, the broader communities in which they operated, and the work itself. I learned a lesson from this, and although it took me a hell of a long time to realize it, it was a very important lesson—maybe one of the most important things I've learned about working relationships and relationships in general: If you want a relationship, *you have to invest.*

For an anthropologist, an outsider's perspective is an invaluable analytical tool. Standing outside provides a vantage into the patterns of practice and thought that animate everyday life, so intrinsic and subtle that they go without saying to the insider. But wanderers don't generally form the kinds of relationships I describe in this book while they drift in and out of people's lives, homes, and businesses. There are certain things you can only really obtain and appreciate by putting down some roots and throwing your lot in with other people, for better or for worse. Relationships, I firmly believe, are one of those things.

In my dissertation, which served as the pilot for this book (and which is available through the UNC library and is a slog), I looked at how craftspeople—and creative professionals more broadly—are able to perform the work they do and how they use that performance to their advantage. That was cool, but I'm less interested now in how people work than I am in *why* people work and what motivates them to keep working beyond the initial honeymoon period of "OMG I got the job!!!!1!!" I argue that working relationships are the *why*.

Working relationships

Working relationships are the intimate connections that individuals develop with their occupations. They are our personal and interpersonal relationships to work. In one dimension, working relationships are **relationships to the work itself**; the worker's connection to the work they do. This includes how they feel about the work (does it make them happy, proud, stressed, worried) and how the work makes them feel (tired, embarrassed, fulfilled, powerful). We naturally explore our relationship to the work itself when we consider whether we like what we do. And whether someone else likes what they do. Do we, or they, hate it? Is it hard? Exciting? Boring? Every time we ask a child what they want to be when they grow up, we are asking them to imagine what sort of occupation they would like to form a relationship with. When we specialize in school or pursue advanced training, we are envisioning what sort of relationship to work would be the most feasible, profitable, enjoyable, and ultimately sustainable for us in the long term.

In a second dimension, working relationships are **relationships to the people with whom someone works**. These are your connections to your coworkers, but coworker in a very broad and inclusive sense. We form working relationships with colleagues, leaders, shareholders, customers, vendors, and anyone else someone comes into contact with during the course of their work. These people contribute to the everyday context in which people perform the work itself. Coworkers can, if you want to extend it out even further, include all of the people who make your working life possible. If you have a spouse, for example, regardless of whether they have a career of their own, their domestic labor directly contributes to your ability to labor outside the home. For the purposes of this book, however, I will focus specifically on the people most intimate to our working lives: leaders, colleagues, and customers.

In a third dimension, and most broadly, working relationships are **relationships to the organizations in which we work**. These can include departments, companies, guilds, industries, markets, and economies. We form working relationships with institutions that are directly or indirectly responsible for compensating us for our work, whether that compensation is money, camaraderie, or recognition. That individuals are able to form relationships to organizations is well established. For example, mission statements, company visions, and value sets are attempts to define the ideal relationship between the company and the individual employee, and between that employee and customers or others with whom they will interact while representing the company. Citizens United determined that businesses were entities capable of forming relationships to political organizations, and were free to act on those relationships in the form of campaign contributions. Many of us develop intense relationships with professional sports organizations. In these pages, I will focus specifically on the relationships individual workers form to the organizations they work for, and to the industries in which they work; e.g., a marketing strategist's connection to their agency, and that strategist's connection to the Work Tech market.

I call these *working* relationships because, obviously, they have to do with work. They are relationships that occur in, around, and with the work that we do. I prefer working relationships to professional relationships, as working relationships are more inclusive of the broader, diverse kinds of relationships we form to labor. Professional relationships tend to describe the connections we form along career tracks, the sort of folks we would follow on LinkedIn, see at industry conferences, and—once upon a time—exchange business cards with. In other words, professional relationships are another way of acknowledging the relationships we form to the people with whom we work. Those are important, for sure, but they are only one facet of the complex relationships we form. Professional relationships tend to leave out institutions, for example, and people rarely ever consider their relationships to the actual labor outside of listing skills on a resume or particularly introspective coaching sessions. Professional relationships is such a well-understood and well-used term that I think co-opting it to describe what I'm trying to talk about would just end up causing confusion. Working relationships it is!

I also like the term *working* because it implies that something is in progress, not yet fully formed, not set in stone, open for debate, and amenable to change. Working relationships are fundamentally malleable. While they can be structured by established career tracks and company hierarchies, they aren't hard-locked. The relationships we form to work, to colleagues, and to companies are flexible, open to interpretation and redirection. A major objective of this book is to show how working relationships can be effectively shaped by intentional investment and intervention. They are something we can *work on*. People leaders spend much of their day working on these relationships, trying to organize teams and generate company culture. There are entire Work Tech categories devoted to improving working relationships: employee engagement, employee experience, rewards and recognition, compensation, well-being (or wellness or total health—whatever that category wants to call itself this year). Having worked professionally with companies and their solutions in all of these categories, I see a common ethos: They believe that working relationships *can* be worked on, *should* be worked on, and, if properly worked on, *will get better*. There is a hopefulness in this ethos that I appreciate and acknowledge: Working relationships—at least good working relationships—are hopeful in that they have the potential to be different. If this wasn't the case, there wouldn't really be a point in studying working relationships at all.

We form working relationships intentionally and unintentionally. You can actively develop skills relevant to your field, aggressively network, and strive to be a "company man" as my grandpa used to say. But even if you turtle up at work and put zero effort into cultivating your relationships, you'll still form working relationships. Humans are social creatures by nature. We can't help but form relationships with people and places and things. Even the most introverted of us. Anyone who has ever worked a part-time job in an industry they don't really care about just to make pocket money or pay bills on the way to something better has probably experienced this phenomenon: You're working a bullshit job at a pizza place, just showing up and putting in your hours, and three months in the manager moves you from the dishwasher to rolling dough. You've (1) just been promoted because you proved your value to your team and the organization, and (2) now you're learning a new skill directly related to your industry. While you were showing up and doing the work necessary to keep earning a paycheck, your working relationships to the pizza place and the pizza industry were developing in the background. My point is, if you're wondering whether you have working relationships, you do. Definitely.

Working relationships and employee experience

Working relationships form the weft and weave of our working lives. Everything comes down to these relationships, and everything is the product of these relationships. That probably sounds pretty grandiose, but I think it bears weight. As fundamentally social creatures, humans see the world through a lens of relationships. It's how we talk about our experience. And it's how a growing literature and thought leadership chorus talks about the *employee* experience in particular. When analysts and organizations talk about employee experience or customer experience, what they are really referring to is *working relationships at scale*. Engagement, well-being, recognition, compensation, all the aspects—or point solutions—that fall under the employee experience Work Tech category are just fancy ways of explaining what happens when particular working relationships fire or misfire.

Approaches to influencing employee and customer experience often leverage relationships implicitly or explicitly. Gartner defines employee experience as the way in which employees internalize and interpret the interactions they have with their organization, as well as the context that underlies those interactions.[4] Gallup describes it as the journey an employee takes with an organization.[5] Bret Starr defines employee, customer, and shareholder experience as the quality of time that someone spends with a brand. For an employee, this includes the whole hire-to-retire/fire life cycle, but also includes the candidate's experience of filling out an application and sitting for interviews, as well as the offboarding experience, where the employee will go after they leave the company and how they'll remember (and recommend) their past employer.[6]

Experience is a useful concept, and these definitions help make sense of a complex phenomenon. Arguing to replace one term with another is a tried-and-true tactic of academic writing and thought leadership more broadly, but it's kind of a bullshit tactic. If the term isn't broken, don't fix it. Experience isn't broken, but it can be

---

[4] From Gartner's Human Resources Glossary, "Employee experience." (see: https://www.gartner.com/en/human-resources/glossary/employee-experience)

[5] Gallup mobilizes this interpretation of employee experience in its consulting service (see: https://www.gallup.com/workplace/242252/employee-experience.aspx)

[6] See Bret Starr's A Humble Guide to Fixing Everything In Brand, Marketing, And Sales (2023).

double-clicked on to increase our understanding of and appreciation for what's going on in such a rich subject. As an anthropologist, I'm partial to a boots-on-the-ground perspective. In this book, and in my own practice, I focus on working relationships rather than employee or customer experience because I want to get down to the most fundamental or grassroots element of experience: the relationships to labor, people, and institutions that weave everyday working (or buying, or shareholding) lives.

I also believe, based on observation and practical experience, that **relationships are the most accessible aspect of employee experience** for individuals to articulate and for others to influence. Relationships are the context through which employees interpret their experience. Relationships are what they encounter on the journey. Relationships are the things with which someone engages during their time with a brand. Experience is a heady concept. Like many theories, it can be vague. Relationships are tangible in a way that experience is not. For example, when you ask someone to describe their employee experience, they will often talk about pain points with certain tools or processes, conflict or camaraderie with coworkers or supervisors, and (dis)connection with the company mission or values. These are all relationships. Likewise, when we devise (or advise) strategies to change or improve employee experience, we often work through the medium of relationships: We implement new tools or processes, we reconfigure teams, we update internal messaging. These may have an impact on overall employee experience, but they do so because they aim to reshape working relationships.

An important throughline of this book is to focus on what you *can* control. Experience is really, really big. I've worked with a lot of business leaders and HR professionals who find the concept difficult to work with because of its scale and because it seems to incorporate everything under the sun (or fluorescent lights). But just like a complex math problem, you can break the seemingly indecipherable string of numbers and letters and squiggly lines into distinct, easier-to-process functions: this plus that or this divided by that. Do each function in turn, and eventually you've solved the equation (or at least made valiant progress toward completing it). Experience works the same way. If you break it down into the discrete threads of the relationships that form experience—your relationship to that kind of work, or that colleague's relationship to their team—positively impacting employee experience or customer experience becomes much more manageable.

All of that said, if you prefer experience over relationships, that's great. You do you. As an anthropologist and a practitioner, I find it valuable to work with the source code of those relationships. If you want to convert the following pages into a work about experience for your own personal headcanon, just add "at scale" after every instance of "working relationship(s)" and you should be golden.

The elemental threads of working relationships— continuity, reciprocity, purpose, and hope

If you can break experience down into a weave of relationships, you can then look closer at that weave and see the individual threads that make up the fabric. Not to spoil it, but the elements that determine the character and quality of our working relationships are continuity, reciprocity, purpose, and hope.

In a craft brewery, the importance of relationships and their constituent elements becomes immediately—sometimes painfully—obvious. With relatively meager salaries, dubious job security, and a scrappy work ethos, American craft breweries float on an artisan's aesthetic of dedication to the craft, investment in supporting and contributing to the "local" and artisanal communities, and their personal perception of what is a fun or cool job.[7] In a stand-up fight with a corporate IT job, even the largest craft breweries can't hope to compete in terms of salary, benefits packages, and air conditioning. Even so, during my research and professional tenure, I saw numerous craft breweries pull IT professionals away from their cushy desk jobs

---

[7] See Delgaty and Wilson's "Craft brewing's hiring crisis, and the challenges of a 'passion-driven' career," Fast Company (2022).

and fill boots on a brewhouse production floor. The opportunity to make something cool, to be part of a cool community, and have a cool lifestyle was enough to compensate for a significant cut in total compensation and the discomfort of sweating over a boiling kettle in the North Carolina summer. (At least for a while.)

At the same time, artisanal businesses were sustained by complex webs of interdependence that were sometimes transactional, but were often more personal than business with a capital "B." Of course, a brewer needs bartenders to pour the beers, customers to buy pints, and city officials to sign off on permits. Brewers need farmers to grow barley and yeast to metabolize sugar into ethanol. They need economies to convert that alcohol into capital and profit. But breweries, like all businesses—and especially small businesses—need tons of informal relationships to function and thrive. I already talked about volunteer labor in a previous section, which was and continues to be essential for breweries to compensate for momentary or seasonal production spikes—e.g., canning runs, festivals—without resorting to contract labor or adding full-time staff. American craft breweries also rely on reciprocal networks with other breweries to borrow, lend, and exchange ingredients or knowledge in a pinch. It is not uncommon, for example, for a brewery to lend a bag of grain or hops to a neighboring establishment that is ostensibly their competitor. Nor would it be odd for a brewer to share the recipe for a particularly good IPA if asked. That's just being neighborly. You can imagine similar informal relationships that drive your own industry or organization: When was the last time you made a purchase decision based purely on product specifications and cost? Often purchasing decisions, like promotion decisions or decisions on where to allocate training budget, are based as much if not more on our feelings—our relationship to the individual or the brand—as much as their qualifications and proven output.

But just because these relationships exist outside of formal contracts doesn't mean they come without cost. We invest a lot in creating, maintaining, and growing these relationships. And when we neglect any of the relationships that drive our work experience, formal or informal, explicit or tacit, we risk disaster.

How do we know then whether we have a good thing going? The devil is in the details. Specifically, in how well we and those with whom we form relationships cultivate continuity, reciprocity, purpose, and hope.

I've spent the last decade engaging in working relationships of my own (as a student, instructor, brewer, researcher, and strategist), but also analyzing them from the outside as a curious observer. In watching so many of these relationships progress over time, I wondered specifically what makes a working relationship succeed or fail. Why do some working relationships initially thrive, only to burn out? Why are some organizations able to maintain long tenures, while others rapidly churn employees? What is the qualitative difference between a promoter eNPS respondent and a detractor?

Being deconstruction-y by nature, I looked for the fundamental elements of working relationships, the constituent parts that, when tweaked, would result in a noticeable change in the working relationship one way or another. I ultimately settled on four (three or five would have been cleaner numbers, but—as I note later—you have to work with what you get): **continuity, reciprocity, purpose, and hope**. Each plays a distinct and vital role in shaping the quality and perceptions of our connections to labor, people, and institutions. The next four sections define these elemental threads and explore their impact on working relationships in greater detail, and offer some lines of questioning to help diagnose whether these elements are functioning or malfunctioning in your experience, but for those with places to go and people to see, here is the TL;DR version:

Continuity is the confidence that a working relationship will remain sustainable and dependable over time. It's the belief, backed by empirical evidence (a long tenure, a storied brand, a set of valuable skills), that your relationship to the work, the people, and the organization will be able to weather the ups and downs of working life. If you don't wake up every morning actively worrying that you will lose your job, you have continuity. If you can see your position being relevant 10 years from now, you have continuity. If it seems like someone is leaving your company every week, you probably don't have continuity (and neither do they).

Once upon a time, you could work at the same company until retirement. Thirty years and a gold watch. Lifelong employment has largely fallen out of fashion and feasibility, but we can still find continuity. It now just plays out on a smaller scale, with five years being a major accomplishment and younger generations of professionals more comfortable with job-hopping and maintaining consistency through a set of marketable skills and a robust book of business.

Reciprocity is the feeling that working relationships are not purely transactional, but sustained by mutual care. Reciprocal relationships are characterized by an equitable give and take. Equitability is an important distinction here: It's not that the exchange of things is strictly fair—i.e., you get one and I get one—but rather that things are given, received, and reciprocated in a way that ultimately balances to the satisfaction of both parties.

Good working relationships are fundamentally reciprocal. The time and effort put into learning a trade or a skill is repaid by being satisfying, by being a source of pride, and by leading to compensation. In the workplace, discretionary effort is rewarded with a bonus or a promotion or a pizza party (hopefully not always the latter). Employers who invest in professional development see better retention, better customer satisfaction, and better engagement.[8] Just like with exchanging gifts with friends or family at the holidays, our feelings of commitment to and affinity for a working relationship is sustained by give-and-take performances that illustrate who we care about, and who cares about us. A relationship that invests in us is one worth investing in.

---

[8] A major finding from LinkedIn Learning's 2018 "Workplace Learning Report," the correlation between greater employer investment and better employee outcomes has been demonstrated in subsequent studies within and across industries at various scales. This oft-repeated revelation has taken on greater significance for talent-strapped businesses in the post-pandemic candidate's market, even if it has not prompted widespread action.

Purpose is the sense that your working relationship is meaningful. For a working relationship to be meaningful, it has to make a desirable impact on you, your family, your organization, or your community. Preferably, all of the above. Our sense of purpose is internally driven, but externally validated. We are personally responsible for figuring out what gives our lives meaning—no leader or mission statement can fill the purpose-shaped hole in your heart. However, we can only really determine whether our purpose was realized by external validation. If we work to save the whales, for example, our purpose is only validated if a whale is saved, or at least safer than they were before our efforts. If we work for the money—which is a perfectly fine purpose, by the bye—but we don't receive that money, chances are we won't maintain that working relationship for very long.

Who cares? What does it all mean? Is it worth it? You've probably wrestled with these questions at some point in your career. You might be wrestling with them now—if so, it's good you're reading this! They are important questions. The answers to these questions are complex and multifaceted—more likely you have numerous intertwined purposes than a single purpose. But figuring out your purpose is absolutely essential to developing a sustainable, resilient relationship to work. If you don't know why you do what you do, you probably won't be able to keep it, especially when the going gets tough and the incentives to stop pile up.

Hope is the optimistic belief that things can change for the better. If you've ever stopped in the middle of a hectic project, taken a breath, and thought, "We'll get through this, everything is going to work out, we've got this," that is hope in action. Humans are fundamentally hopeful creatures. We need to imagine the light at the end of the tunnel in order to keep walking through the darkness. Hope is also active. It's not just imagining the light, but also taking the step. Hope is the will to pursue that change, despite the odds. When CEOs give keynote speeches on drive or grit, what they're really talking about is hope in action—the willingness to push through hardship because you believe there is something better on the other side.

Hope is very squishy. It's probably not something that many think about in the workplace, at least not in for-profit companies. But I would argue that hope is the most important of the elements for creating resilient working relationships. If we did not believe at some fundamental, if unspoken, level that the work we were doing could make a difference, bring about change, or create a better world for ourselves and those we love—even in some small way—why would we even bother getting out of bed? Having struggled with depression my whole life, I, and many others like me, can relate to hopelessness. The absence of hope is real, and it sucks. But by knowing what it feels like to lose hope, you can also appreciate how inspiring it is, how much momentum it creates, when hope returns. Resilient working relationships are hopeful, and good working relationships create spaces that encourage hopefulness.

Why working relationships matter

You may be saying at this point, "That's all well and good, Mr. Scientist, but how do we know this isn't all just theoretical mumbo-jumbo?" Indeed, in order to have practical value, working relationships need to be impactful. The good news is that well-crafted working relationships directly contribute to employee engagement and resilience, which in turn impact the profitability and stability of the organizations to which each party belongs. However, for these relationships to be engaging and resilient, certain conditions need to be met. Namely, continuity, reciprocity, purpose, and hope need to be present in the relationship and actively maintained. A deficit in any one of these factors can lead to significant stress in the relationship. If this deficit continues or spreads to other elements, the relationship will collapse.

A matter of engagement

Good working relationships inspire engagement. In interviews, leaders who boasted of strong employee experience, employees who readily endorsed their employer in eNPS surveys and referrals, and organizations with above-average employee tenures, and CEOs who experienced growth in recession economies consistently spoke about working relationships that were consistent, reciprocal, purposeful, and hopeful. These were the relationships that could be counted on; no one would walk in one day to find their keycard didn't work or their online credentials revoked. These were relationships that rewarded hard work. These were relationships that gave lives meaning, that provided for families and souls. These were relationships that could—and regularly did—move upward and onward.

Do you remember the early days of the COVID-19 pandemic? Watching *Tiger King* on Netflix, looking for cool furniture in trees in *Animal Crossing*, and ordering contactless delivery at an absurd markup? I remember. If you also worked during that period of time, or immediately after, you probably also remember how awful employee engagement was at the time for so many workers. Whether you still worked in person or worked remotely, there was a pronounced listlessness in the professional world. Anxiety over lockdown and infection rates, widespread layoffs and supply chain issues, and a general sense of uncertainty during a once-in-a-lifetime event did not do wonders for the working spirit. Reddit posts, TikToks, and later mainstream news outlets began reporting more and more on the general malaise and angst of the professional class. Front-line workers, who saw their situation go from bad to worse, were also very understandably *over it*, but left with significantly fewer options. Overall, there was an almost oppressive sense of "why bother?" It was a time of peak disengagement.

Seeing the problem and sensing disaster, some organizations decided to throw out conventions in an effort to save engagement. One organization I encountered was particularly successful. A marketing agency headquartered in Fort Worth, Texas, took several radical steps. First, they went "remote by default," meaning that any employee at the organization, no matter their role or how close they lived to the office, could work remotely as often as they wanted. All meetings would be held over Zoom so that nobody would be left out. Second, they implemented several wellness initiatives in an effort to take pressure off of employees who were adjusting to the pandemic lifestyle. This included switching to a four-day workweek, establishing two hours of "quiet time" every day where employees could reliably work without being pinged or emailed, and offering a weekly stipend for meal delivery services like Hello Fresh. Third, in order to stay connected, they sent all of the employees a VR headset. That was just cool. Finally, and perhaps most important, agency leadership committed to not laying anyone off during the pandemic. Surrounded by rampant downsizing in the professional services space, you can imagine the impact this promise had.

The impact on engagement was undeniable. eNPS scores shot up and stayed up. Employees reported more productivity, more job satisfaction, and less stress. Customer success was at an all-time high. Employees were saving money by not having to commute or purchase professional clothing. They had more time to spend in deep work, and with their families. There was an overall sense that work was fun. I analyzed the company's employee experience surveys from 2021 and 2022 as part of my application to the company. The results I found were so convincing that, when they offered me a job three months later, I accepted on the spot.

Given the fuzzy nature of relationships, I've found qualitative research to be the greatest source of insight into the qualities of resilient working relationships and their impact on individual lives and organizational success. However, quantitative studies suggest a correlation between high continuity, reciprocity, purpose, and hope organizations and strong performance in internal and external key performance indicators (KPIs), including improvement in employee performance, retention, and customer satisfaction. Engagement is the big KPI, and it serves as something of an umbrella measurement or bellwether for performance, retention, and satisfaction. Engagement is also the most cited result of a good employee experience (which is the result of strong working relationships!)—a good employee experience creates engaged employees. Gallup's 2023 State of the Global Workplace report found that 85% of employees are either not engaged in their work or actively disengaged in their work. I'm not entirely sure what the distinction is between being "not engaged" and "actively disengaged," but it's not hard to believe. If you've been in a conference room or on a Zoom call in the last year, the apathy is palpable.

To be fair, I don't believe the pandemic is to blame for the current engagement crisis. It certainly didn't do employees and employers any favors, but the seeds for a disconnected workforce were planted long before the first lockdown: precarious employment, stagnated wages, rampant corporate corruption, and a general sense that the next generation's quality of life would, in fact, *not* be better than the previous generation's. After earning my bachelor's degree in 2009, graduate school seemed like a much more viable option than the disaster that was the post-2008 housing crash economy. 2012 only cemented this conviction, and 2020 came in for the hat trick. Working relationships were hard to start, hard to cultivate, hard to sustain, and ultimately hard to invest in.

Understandable as it is, broken engagement is generating a huge revenue loss for organizations, costing over $450 billion annually.[9] Retention sucks: While quit rates hit an all-time high in 2021 (an interesting rebound to the mass layoffs of 2020), things have not improved much. As of 2023, over half of employees are considering leaving their job within a year.[10] Even before the pandemic, 33% of professionals reported walking away from their jobs because they were *bored*.[11] Even though research reports have celebrated high rates

---

[9] This according to a 2013 Gallup study by Susan Sorenson and Keri Garman. Given more recent economic precarity and the increased sophistication of engagement measurement techniques and data collection, this figure has likely grown significantly over the past decade.

[10] See Huileng Tan's "More than half of U.S. workers want to quit their jobs in 2023, a new survey shows," Business Insider (2023).

[11] It's an older code, but it checks out. See "Breaking Boredom: Job Seekers Jumping Ship for New Challenges in 2018," from Korn Ferry.

of employee satisfaction—51% are extremely or very satisfied with their job overall—these same studies acknowledge that satisfaction varies considerably based on income, position, industry, and age.[12] Statistics like this are also always double-sided: If 51% of respondents are extremely satisfied with their jobs, what's going on with the other 49%? Why aren't things better for them?

Conversely, the benefits of an engaged team are well documented with big statistics. Engaged employees are 23% more profitable, they achieve 10% greater customer satisfaction, and contribute 18% less turnover at high-turnover organizations and 43% less turnover at low-turnover organizations.[13] Employees who have development opportunities are dramatically less likely to job hop.[14] I ran a series of studies between 2022 and 2023 for several employee engagement, learning, and professional development platforms in an attempt to showcase the return on investment of their methodologies and solutions. Across the studies, we found that employers who reported growth in 2022 and 2023, and who projected growth in 2024 and beyond, were significantly more likely to report that their employees were engaged. These same organizations actively invested in creating positive employee experiences, in expanding and diversifying employee development opportunities (including promotions, upskilling, and reskilling), and in consistently recognizing and rewarding employees who went above and beyond.

What is also interesting is that employees surveyed in these same studies who reported working for growing companies were also 30% more likely on average to characterize their employee experience as having continuity, reciprocity, purpose, and hope than employees of organizations that did not invest in employee experience. These same

---

[12] See Juliana Menasce Horowitz and Kim Parker's 2023 study for the Pew Research Center, "How Americans View Their Jobs."

[13] See Gallup's "The Benefits of Employee Engagement" (2023).

[14] From Kim Parker and Juliana Menasce Horowitz's "Majority of workers who quit a job in 2021 cite low pay, no opportunities for advancement, feeling disrespected" (2022), Pew Research Center.

employees were significantly more likely to feel motivated by their work, to feel valued by their companies, and to be content in their current organization, and significantly more likely to recommend their employer to a friend even if they were no longer working at that company.

What I have consistently found, in both qualitative and quantitative data sets, is that feeling that your working relationship is likely to continue, that your efforts are equitably rewarded, that the work you do is meaningful to you and others, and that things can and will get better if you keep pushing toward that goal, inspires an engaged employee. It makes sense. If you feel that your working relationship is worth your while—and one that has continuity, reciprocity, purpose, and hope in adequate measure that is demonstrably worthwhile—you are much more likely to engage in that relationship and the work, people, and organizations it entails.

A matter of resilience

Good working relationships create resilient people, organizations, and communities. Resilience is the capacity of an organism (or organization) to absorb change and still maintain its essential functioning. Less technically, **resilience is the capacity to roll with change rather than being rolled by change**. Resilient employees are able to adapt to changing conditions, handle the pressures of changing times, and exceed expectations that employers have for them and that they have for themselves. Resilient organizations are able to stay agile and thrive in spite of market volatility. Resilient communities persist.

Each elemental thread contributes to the resilience of working relationships, and thus the resilience of the people, organizations, and communities within those relationships, in its own way. Continuity stokes the confidence needed to rise against challenges. Reciprocity ties people together in mutual affinity. Purpose is the north star that guides us through the darkness. Hope is the motivation to keep getting up after getting knocked down, to keep going even when the challenge seems insurmountable.

As I discuss in a later chapter, good working relationships also have a resiliency of their own. When working relationships have continuity, reciprocity, purpose, and hope in adequate amounts, they are able to survive the expected and unexpected storms of working life: interpersonal disputes, bad client experiences, economic downturns, layoffs, pandemics. Elements within working relationships can also compensate for the degradation or absence of another: Job security can offset the angst of a salary freeze, or the potential of a new career can assuage the fear of starting over.

The world of work is constantly changing. The pandemic, the Great Resignation, and all the other major and minor crises of the past several years did not create a "new normal." What they have revealed is that there is no such thing as normal, insofar as normal is a synonym for stable. Instability is the true norm. Resiliency should be a top priority for individuals and their organizations, because an absence of resilience is disaster.

Creating resilient relationships is a never-ending practice. Even the most resilient relationships—like the most resilient organisms or organizations—have their limit. Disengagement. Disconnection. Apathy. Burnout. These are all warning signs of a vulnerable working relationship, a vulnerable employee, business, or industry. They are also the direct result of neglecting the continuity, reciprocity, purpose, or hope of our relationships to work. The good news is that these relationships, while sensitive, are also highly mendable. Even if your working relationships—your employee experience, your engagement, your resilience—are looking bleak right now, you can fix it. If you invest in creating the conditions in which strong working relationships can thrive, they will.

Focusing on the elements of working relationships that are within your locus of control is critical. Investing in better understanding your own relationships to work, to the people with whom you work, and to the organizations for which you work is an important first step to determining what you want from these relationships, what is within your control to change, and the best next steps you can take to achieve that ideal. This book is about taking that first step on the road to resilience by asking yourself, and answering: *What is the quality of your working relationships?*

Is this book for you?

I hope so. In all seriousness, there are three profiles of readers that I believe would find an introduction to an internal and collective dialogue about working relationships useful.

First, this book is intended for the individual reader who finds themselves chronically unhappy with their work situation, but is unsure why or where they should start fixing it. While I can't offer a step-by-step guide on how to create a better working relationship— our relationships to work are deeply personal, and while what works for me may work for you, discovering the key to a resilient working relationship is an important quest that only you can take—this book will help you develop a deeper understanding of their connection to work. If you've ever paused in the flow of work and wondered what this is all about, why do we bother with all of this, why you get out of bed every morning and perform a job, this book explores and illustrates a series of ideas about working relationships that can set you on a path to answering these questions for yourself.

Likewise, if you are already on the experience bus, but want to better understand the underlying dynamics that shape that experience for better and for worse, I think you'll find this book useful. If you've ever been prepping for a lunch service, writing out a lesson plan, or staring at a spreadsheet and wondered at an existential level, "What the fuck am I doing? What are any of us doing?" I think a deep dive into the ins and outs of working relationships will be very satisfying.

Second, this book is for leaders who believe in the importance of experience in the world of work, but struggle to diagnose what specifically is functioning or malfunctioning in their employee experience or where they should start. The first section of this book introduces each of the concepts in turn, and then holistically as the foundation of our working relationships. The last chapter offers a do-it-yourself set of ethnographic questions that you can use to open a dialogue with yourself and then with your employees and colleagues. Again, this book is neither a *top 10 tips* listicle nor a self-help guide. Rather, it's the start of a conversation that you will need to continue long beyond the last page. (If you are in this camp, I highly recommend that you start approaching the concepts and questions in this book first as an individual reader. You won't be able to understand much about your employees' or colleagues' relationships to work if you don't first have a solid grasp of the strengths and weaknesses of your own.)

Finally, this book is for experienced skeptics who, while familiar with the concepts of employee or customer experience, are still on the fence about the practical value of such a seemingly nebulous concept. I can appreciate that. In a moment when pressures are high and budgets are tight, nobody wants to spend their money—and their reputation—on a big question mark. My goal then, even if you don't take up the dialogue for yourself, is to illustrate the tangible impact of experience through the more accessible lens of working relationships. As squishy as these concepts may seem, they do matter. Productivity, retention, eNPS-style satisfaction, and revenue—metrics that seem so clean and quantifiable in a spreadsheet or quarterly report—are in reality only shorthand for the connections that individuals form—or don't—to the work they do, the people with whom they work, and the organizations for which they work.

However, even if after reading all of this you still feel in your heart of hearts that employee experience is a COVID-19-era fad, that all your organization needs to be more resilient is for workers to stop whining and just be happy they have jobs, or that a pizza party will solve your engagement problem, this book is not for you.

What's to come

In the coming pages, I explore the elemental threads of working relationships—continuity, reciprocity, purpose, and hope—in greater detail. I define each element, explore its significance in the context of work, how it impacts our working relationships and broader experience of work for better and for worse, and some practical strategies for improving each element in your own practice and in the working lives of others. Stepping a level up, I'll then consider the intersection of these elements, how they work with and against one another to shape the character and quality of our working relationships, and how they contribute to the overall durability and vulnerability of working relationships. I end with a practical diagnostic for evaluating the character and quality of your working relationships and those of your organization.

You will notice that this book doesn't really offer advice. Like I noted above, this isn't a self-help book or self-actualization guide from a power CEO. I'm not far enough along in my own career or in my own life to have that sort of advice to give. Instead, what I can offer are the same ethnographic questions that I use to better understand the challenges, pressures, opportunities, and organizational and interpersonal dynamics that shape our experiences of work. Good research happens *within* context. I don't know your context, but I can share with you the research techniques—the ways of digging into a lived experience, picking it up, and turning it around in your hands to see the various angles—that have allowed me to write this book and to make sense of my own journey.

This book is structured like a story in that each chapter builds toward a climax, a look at the situation on the ground followed by a "so what" explaining the significance of it and the questions you can ask or steps you can take to confront your own experience. At the same time, fondly remembering the Choose Your Own Adventure genre of books that had a moment when I was growing up in the '90s, I have endeavored to equip each section of the book, each subtitle within each chapter, with its own "so what." I have also tried to avoid being overly self-referential to other sections of the book (e.g., "as I talked about in chapter three"). I'm not the book police—read it however you want.

I will ask, however, that if you are reading this book in a linear fashion, to participate in some self-guided research. More and more, thought leaders and practitioners in the world of work advocate measurement and tracking to determine the ROI of an engagement. By way of benchmarking your own experience, please consider this question before reading on:

On a scale of zero to 10, with zero being not at all and 10 being extremely, how resilient is your relationship to work?

THE ELEMENTAL THREADS
OF WORKING RELATIONSHIPS

CONTINUITY

*Continuity is the trust that underwrites
enduring working relationships.*

Defining continuity

In a chaotic world, we crave continuity. Even those restless types who constantly seek new stimulation want consistency at some level in some aspects of their lives. Constant all-encompassing change is not sustainable. Nor is it desirable. We seek continuity in our personal relationships: We learn to predict our partner's moods. We find enjoyment in predicting what gifts will surprise and delight our friends on their birthdays. We depend on reliable parents. The same is true in the professional world; resilient working relationships have continuity.

Continuity is not stagnation. It's not the absence of change. That would be monotonous and antithetical to hope, which, as we'll talk about later, is the optimism for change. Rather, continuity is a pattern. We expect the seasons to change, but to do so in a particular order. There can be—and often is—variation within the pattern; some summers are hotter than others, some winters colder. But the fact that summer follows spring and spring follows winter is stable. In a relationship, working or otherwise, **continuity is our confidence that we can anticipate what will happen next in a relationship with a reasonable degree of consistency**. Continuity is the **trust** we have that the thing to which we form a working relationship, be it the work, the people, or the organization, won't unexpectedly coldcock us. Sure, relationships surprise us all the time, for better and for worse.

That's life. But a relationship in which conditions are consistently unpredictable, in which it is routinely unclear how to win or what will result in a loss, where you don't know whether you are building toward something or wasting your time, is not healthy. Working relationships without continuity are not sustainable.

Continuity sketches out the cadence and boundaries of our working relationships. In the broadest sense, relationships are patterns. These patterns are what we can expect from an interaction: From a family member, we expect acceptance; from an employer, we expect payment; from a coworker, we expect a round of drinks at Charlie's after work on Thursday and a heavy session of shit-talking. We develop our relationships by responding to these patterns in ways that are also predictable; we continually show up for work, interact with colleagues, submit paperwork on time (or mostly on time), and participate in the drinking and shit-talking. Being at least reasonably predictable is how we get experience, establish tenure, and build a reputation. Without some degree of continuity, we wouldn't really have working relationships at all.

The nature of continuity in a working relationship—or what a predictable professional pattern looks like—has changed considerably over the last several decades. Once upon a time, continuity in the workplace was going down to the local car factory, getting a job (with a firm handshake), working up through the company for 40-odd years, and retiring. Lifetime employment, from hire to retire, was both the gold standard and the expectation for many across industries, blue or white collar, working or professional class. This was true not only in the United States, but in other major capitalist economies like Japan, where sarariman corporate culture, with its company-man ethos and escalator promotions, was considered a pinnacle of professional success.[15]

---

[15] Anthropologist of Japan Anne Allison has written extensively about the rise and collapse of lifelong employment in Japan, and the downstream effects of this broken promise on the professional prospects and emotional well-being of younger Japanese (see Allison 2013).

Now, lifelong employment is largely extinct, the baby boomers being the last generation to have considerable experience with the phenomenon, even as forced early retirements cut their careers short. The advent of cheap offshore production, flexible labor models, and myriad technological innovations has disincentivized employers from retaining expensive long-tenured employees. Developing a 30-year-long relationship doesn't seem practical in a world of contract hires and other forms of temporary employment. At the same time, even for organizations that would like to keep the dream of long tenures alive, macroeconomic uncertainties have encouraged, and just as often necessitated, rampant layoffs. My grandpa used to talk about being laid off as something akin to a scarlet letter. Now, being laid off, having a work gap, or pivoting to a different industry is common for Gen Xers and younger generations. It's not so much a matter of *if* you will unexpectedly lose your job, but *when*.

But the demise of lifelong employment has not lessened the desire for or importance of continuity in working relationships. Rather, just as employers have shifted their practices and priorities, employees have shifted how they interpret continuity, and where they seek it.

For employers and employees, continuity is still measured in terms of tenure. Previously, the ideal tenure was hire-to-retire, lifelong. Now, the ideal (read: feasible) tenure is a "long" one. "Long" is conveniently subjective; the age of precarious employment has necessitated that what qualifies as "long" be fairly malleable depending on economic conditions, industry trends, and the career conventions of employees from different generations. Depending on who, where, and when, "long" may mean 20 years or even a decade. I worked with an agency that inducted employees into a secret society-esque "inner ring," complete with an actual ring, on their five-year anniversary. I've interviewed numerous CEOs and VPs about their organizational culture who have bragged about the number of employees who have "been here from the start," often glossing over the fact that the "start" was only two or three years ago.

Employers also look for continuity from their employees. This introduces a whole different set of nuances for "long." Most hiring managers I've met, be they in technology, service, academia, or manufacturing, would raise an eyebrow at a staccato resume full of five- or six-month stints. What is the ideal amount of time you should stay with an employer to seem credible is a question that gets answered in private conversations, on Reddit forums, and in TikTok videos in the same way that people pass around home remedies for a cold or hiccups. Is a year long enough? Two years? If I have had three different employers in the past five years, is that bad? Red flags on a resume are ultimately subjective (and wise employers consider the context of a candidate's employment, not just the length), but a good deal of the will they/won't they of matching a candidate to a position and an employee to an employer comes down to interpretations and evaluations of tenure.

But not everyone plays this kind of tenure game. Nor are they expected to. Independent contractors, freelancers, and others working in the flexible or gig economy measure their success and value in terms of completed contracts. Continuity may come from a steady stream of projects, or a percentage of repeat customers. While I've met plenty who actively seek to escape the gig economy—flexible employment is not for everyone, and not all gig-type jobs are sustainable (and some are downright exploitative)—I've also met many colleagues from all generations—including baby boomers—who appreciate the freedom of not being tied down to a particular employer and getting to be their own boss through a client-consultant, rather than employer-employee, relationship. Some people just like to job hop. If you don't care about setting down roots in an organization and you have the skills to stay in demand, it makes sense to move between organizations or industries as your interests and prospects change. Having job hopped and freelanced myself, I have a degree of nostalgia for the rough-and-tumble days of no-strings-attached employment.[16]

---

[16] "No strings attached" is a bit of a misnomer here. In reality, all working relationships, no matter how temporary, have strings. We'll talk about this in the next chapter.

Having worked on both sides, I've realized that no matter how flexible one's employment may be, we still desire continuity as a fundamental element of our working relationships. If not tenure or a healthy pipeline of contracts, continuity may come from the consistency and stability of an industry or trade. I had a classmate in grad school who quit her anthropology degree and instead got a degree—and eventually a career—in corporate accounting because it wasn't clear to her how marketable anthropology would be and because "no matter what, the world is always going to need accountants." Industry continuity was a drama that played out almost daily in craft brewing. Brewer and business owner interlocutors often cited the history of beer production—a craft stretching back in one form or another to ancient Mesopotamia (or earlier)—as evidence that the industry would never die.

Others based their confidence on the belief that people would always be willing to pay for beer. "It's the only recession-proof industry," an empirically false statement they would nevertheless repeat ad nauseam, claiming that no matter how bad economic conditions became, people would still find the resources to drink away their sadness. [Note that this sentiment completely disregards (1) that people could make their own alcohol, and (2) that, in times of economic hardship, people would be far more likely to buy cheaper macro beer than expensive craft beers.]

On the other side, many were convinced the bottom would fall out of the market at any minute, that this was a terrible investment of resources, time, and skill, and that craft beer would crash again just like it had in the '80s and then again in the '90s. Craft beer doomsdayers would point to fluctuations in the commodities market—an increase in aluminum prices here, a dig in barley production there—or their own taprooms—"It's usually packed on Thursday night!"—as harbingers of an imminent collapse.

It was in the volatile world of American craft brewing, where brewery closures and acquisitions were overshadowed by the scores of new breweries that would open every month, that I encountered professionals who experienced continuity in their working relationships not in the promise of a particular employer or the stability of a particular industry, but through a much more internalized locus of control: their skills, knowledge, and expertise.

You can't control the economy. You don't own the company. Nobody can control the whims of fickle consumers. You can control and own your professional development. You can't guarantee a promotion, but you can build your skills and knowledge through on-the-job learning and after-hours study such that, when the time comes with this employer or another, you'll be ready. Economies can go into recession and jobs can fire you, but nobody can take away your experiences. You get to keep those. And because you get to keep those, no matter what happens in your job or in your world, your skills, knowledge, and expertise become a source of stability in an otherwise consistently chaotic world.

Brewers, especially brewers who did not have equity in their breweries, would often talk about the quality of their beer as their ticket to better employment and sunnier futures. "The owner is an asshole and I hate this brewery," one brewer put it frankly, "but every beer I make for that asshole makes me better at brewing." Every brew brought him one step closer to being able to hop to a much better situation.

Likewise, every contract can bring a freelancer one step closer to full-time employment. Every successful project can bring an employee one step closer to promotion. Every study can bring a researcher one step closer to discovering the big answer. I think it's no coincidence that professional development is the most requested form of employer investment after salary increases. You get to keep both. And development is more durable than money (although development can't immediately pay for a flat tire or school lunch). Skills, knowledge, and experience are an ownable, internalized form of continuity in an otherwise discontinuous world.

I dig deeper into the importance of skills later in this chapter. Suffice to say for now that, whether in the form of tenure, industry affiliation, or skills, continuity is not only desirable, it's critical. In an unpredictable world of work, continuity is the basis on which we assure ourselves that, whatever may happen next, we will be okay. Even if we wake up one morning to a severance email or a thousand-year--old industry suddenly collapses, continuity is the belief that enough binds our working relationships together, be it shared history, mutual affinity, or sheer need of valuable labor, that we will survive. It is the belief, founded on a reasonable degree of certainty, yet never fully certain, that we will endure that weaves resilience into our working relationships.

Partial control

Maintaining continuity in a working relationship is difficult. The reason for this is both straightforward and frustrating: Work is only ever partially in our control. We never work alone. Colleagues, clients, tools, materials, macroeconomic forces, and the environment have lives of their own that shape the work we do and the things we produce. The things we create are never solo productions. These collaborators transform our work in ways beyond our control and in ways that often exceed our expectations and intentions. COVID-19 was a crash course and master class in partial control. A virus radically reshaped the way we worked. Masks, Zoom, and CDC guidelines changed the way we took meetings, collaborated with teammates, or shipped products. For those now working from home, spouses, kids, and pets became part of office culture. The pandemic forced us to look so closely at how much of our working lives could change without our consent, to take an inventory of what we could and could not control. It's no wonder this introspection led to a boom in employee experience discussions and strategies.

"The world of work will never be the same." "No new normal." "VUCA."[17] These post-pandemic headlines position uncertainty and

---

[17] VUCA stands for "volatility, uncertainty, complexity, and ambiguity." The acronym has become increasingly popular among thought leaders and analysts for explaining the challenges of the current working context.

unpredictability as something new. The fact is, though, that change is and always has been the norm. Decades of relative stability are actually an aberration, if they exist at all. People often remember the '70s, '80s, and '90s as periods of success and certainty. Golden ages. Japanese economists and historians of Japan refer to Japan's postwar economic progress as the "economic miracle." However, the nostalgia of better days often obscures the reality of everyday life in the moment. Maybe it was easier to turn a profit or achieve the American (or Japanese) dream in the 1970s. Children also practiced taking cover under their desks in the very real possibility of a nuclear missile strike. If crisis is the potential for things to change, then our lives broadly—and working lives specifically—are always *in crisis*.

Our relationships with work are, and always have been, marked by partial control. Once upon a time, we had to worry about raiders coming over the hills and making off with our livestock, or maybe a rival king sacking our fiefdom and imposing a new tax. Now, our careers can be upended by corporate acquisitions or stock market crashes. Partial control is something we've come to accept, another convention of working life that goes without saying because it comes without saying. Even as we might imagine ourselves as powerful, independent actors, masters of our craft, titans of industry, the fact is that whatever control we actually have is tempered by the influence of things that also have power. This is not to say that we totally lack agency; if we were totally adrift, I doubt we would find work tolerable, let alone enjoyable. Rather, while we exercise a degree of control over our working lives, it is important to be mindful of the power of the things we work *with* and their potential to exceed our control and overwhelm us.

The limitations of our control become most apparent when something in our working lives goes wrong. A popped tire on the way to a big presentation. A colleague swooping and pooping on a project at the last minute. The boss's nephew being promoted over you. We all have hands-on experience with unexpected and undeserved friction and failure. But it's these same moments when things fly out of our hands that underscore the importance of continuity, our trust that, even though some things are up in the air (and some things are totally fucked), we will be okay.

For me, brewing was my first practical seminar in partial control. Before I stepped foot in the production side of a brewery, I mostly worked with theory. My working life revolved around graduate classes, semester grades, and my own research. There were certainly aspects outside of my control, but these variables were relatively few and I was inured to them after decades of formal education. Brewing was different. First, there was a lot I didn't know. It was brand-new territory to me and, outside of what I read in books or watched in videos (which was a poor substitute for the real thing), I had no context for what I or anyone else was doing. Second, brewing involved significantly more collaborators than academia, both human and inhuman. There were coworkers, bosses, local officials, safety and health inspectors, vendors, delivery drivers, landlords, and customers who all had to be satisfied in their own ways. There was the beer itself, fermented by yeast that, as a living organism, had its own needs and quirks that were very hard to read at first (and only slightly less hard to read as I gained experience). Did you know that the taste, color, and alcohol content of a finished beer can vary even if you use the exact same recipe and process every time? I didn't at first, because I didn't realize that micro-variations in the sugar content of barley based on fluctuating variables during the growing season could create very significant variations when used at scale.

Even when you follow the recipe, adjust for the variations, and take all the reasonable precautions, you can still fail. I experienced this firsthand when a thunderstorm nearly ruined my first porter.

I was an intern at the time, and we had brewed on a Friday. It was the storm season in North Carolina, and the local power grid was notoriously susceptible to outages by lightning or strong winds. Like most breweries, we used an electronic cooling system to help regulate the temperature in the fermentor. Fermentation creates heat (in addition to alcohol), and too much heat can make yeast do weird things that can have disastrous effects on the character and quality of the beer. An internal sensor measures the temperature in the tank and pumps coolant through jackets to keep the fermenting beer at an optimal 68°F.

Typically, and especially during the storm season, a brewer would pop in on the weekend to double-check the systems and ensure fermentation was going smoothly. This weekend, however, was one of North Carolina's most prominent beer festivals and beer competitions. We were all heading out of town. The brewery could have designated one of us to stay behind, but the festival was important for professional development and networking, especially important in a community-driven industry like craft beer. Rather than making someone miss out on the opportunity, we decided to risk it.

Probably 99 times out of a 100, it would have been fine. This time, it was not. When a storm rolled through around 11 that night, a questing bolt of lightning overloaded the brewery's power grid, knocking out the electricity for about 30 minutes. When power was restored, the cooling valves should have automatically clicked back on. However, the valve to the porter stuck closed. This caused a chain reaction in the fermenting beer: The liquid got hotter, the yeast got more active, the liquid got even hotter, and then the yeast got stressed and started to get weird. In this case, it generated butyric acid, a compound that occurs in bad fermentations that carries a noticeable flavor and aroma of sour milk.

It was not a complete disaster, but it was pretty close. Twenty-thousand dollars worth of beer tasted weird. It might mellow with time. We could also cut the beer with a strongly flavored additive that might cover up the butyric acid—cold-brewed coffee being the strongest contender. However, this later option would mean we'd have a *coffee porter*—not a porter—on tap, potentially limiting the customer base. There was no guarantee that the coffee would solve the problem. It might make it worse. The head brewer rolled the dice and hoped time would heal all wounds.

The result was a mixed bag. The sour milk notes did mellow

over time as the yeast dropped out of suspension, but they were still noticeable to those with sensitive palates (and those looking for it). A couple of people sent back pints. The beer sold slowly—not uncommon for dark beers in warm climates like North Carolina—but still worrying to the brewing staff who wanted to move the botched beer out of the shop as soon as possible. Some longtime customers said it was the brewery's best porter to date, a frustrating sentiment given that the finished product was an accident and not replicable. The beer had a more significant impact on the brewers; every week, the brewers would pour a pint, sit at the bar, and scowl. They still tasted the defect, and regretted not taking steps to mask the flavor. Ultimately, keeping the beer around became too aggravating; the brewers dumped the last 130-odd gallons of beer down the drain.

You can do everything right on your end, and things can still go to hell. Even if someone had stayed back with the beer, there was no guarantee that anyone would have been able to unstick the valve in time. Sometimes, you just can't win. And that's because you aren't the only one playing the game. As workers, employers, founders, etc., our task is not to control everything. No matter how skilled you are, that's impossible. A more reasonable goal is to try our best in the areas we can impact, and be resilient in navigating the aspects we can't. Continuity in a chaotic world is not control, but rather the confidence that you will be able to roll with that chaos toward creating something worthwhile—a product, a company, a life—even if the creative process is not entirely your own.

Asymmetrical influence

While fundamentally important to the resilience of working relationships, continuity is also fragile. Sometimes, incredibly so. Threats to one's confidence that they will be okay, come what may, come in many forms and in many sizes. A run of difficult customers can cause a barista to lose confidence in her skills. A public relations operative can fall out with their network. A promising business can shutter because of a pandemic. Yet, in terms of frequency and magnitude, employers have a disproportionate impact on continuity. This is especially true for employees who are relatively new in their careers, just beginning to form their working relationships, and have yet to develop the skills, knowledge, and networks needed to ground their confidence in the wider world of work. But even seasoned professionals can be severely shaken when their employers fail to meet employee expectations of stability and reliability.

Employers weigh heavy on continuity in all manner of industries and businesses; as the adage goes "people don't leave bad jobs, they leave bad bosses." People do, in fact, leave bad jobs—I quit a donut shop despite having an awesome boss who used to take us ghost hunting—but the statement nevertheless rings true regarding the importance of good leadership to the overall well-being and resilience of a workforce. Bob Cratchit is relatable because he works for a shitty boss (and because anyone who has ever worked for a Scrooge has likely wished their supervisor would have a similar ghost-induced change of heart). *Office Space's* Bill Lumbergh is infuriating because he is a believable stereotype. "You know what? I quit!" is triumphant and cathartic because we daydream of saying those same words. Look past the embellishments of horrible boss stories that go viral on subreddits and TikTok and you can see a common narrative stretching across the generations in which an out-of-touch, egomaniacal employer serves as the primary villain.

A boss's asymmetrical influence on work experience is both practical and symbolic. It is practical in the sense that managers, directors, C-suite executives, and all manner of leaders *do* have the ability to directly and indirectly impact what an employee can and can't do, when they can do it, with whom, etc., by nature of their position. Telling other people what to do comes with the territory. Their decisions also carry a greater weight. In strategy projects, when clients ask which stakeholders should be involved in the process, we always ask for anyone who can kill the project. There is always one or two or 10 people who, with a word or a facial expression, sink an idea that collaborators lower in the hierarchy float. All opinions might be valid, but some are more valuable than others. Often, these opinions are directly tied to pursestrings or the names on the door. "Who signs your checks?" is a powerful idiom for reasserting the chain of command because someone *does* actually have to sign a check.

A leader's impact is also symbolic. In a world of work that is always outside our full control, it helps to put a face to the aggregate inconveniences and disappointments we encounter. It personalizes the crisis, making our work experience someone's fault, rather than the outcome of bad luck or chaos. The people above you do have relatively more control than you (i.e., they at least get to tell you what to do), so they become a natural outlet for frustration. Why do bad things happen to good people? Because the sales director botched a campaign or the CFO bought a worthless recruiting platform. It might be a thin thread, but it's often better than nothing.

To illustrate the leader's influence as a practitioner and symbol, consider this scenario: A company decides it must lay off 30% of its staff. The executive leadership team assembles and determines which employees they can afford to let go and which they can afford to retain. They announce the layoff on a Tuesday, giving those impacted about three hours' advance notice. The survivors are shocked, sad, confused, angry, a little relieved, fearful. The executive leadership team blames poor sales and a weak economy. They're doing the best they can, but it's either cut some people loose or the whole business collapses. This explanation largely falls on deaf ears. The remaining employees are disgruntled. Employee satisfaction hits an all-time low.

In the following hours, days, and weeks, office discussions invariably turn to rounds of "who's the asshole?" Whose fault ultimately was it that 30% of their colleagues lost their jobs? The reality is that it was a confluence of events, some within and some without human control. The economy was in recession. Changing client needs made some positions redundant. People just aren't spending money.

However, that doesn't change the fact that someone made the choice. Certainly, there were circumstances pressuring the decision.

It could have seemed like the only viable decision. It might even have been the right decision. But that's all academic. At the end of the day, someone with authority did make a decision, and that decision created an unfortunate result. It's understandable to resent the decision, to resent the authority that enabled that decision, and to resent the person who exercised that authority, no matter how much you may be able to see their point of view or the necessity of their action. If you're negatively impacted by the decision, logic or empathy can feel like cold comfort. In a sense, that is the cost leaders pay for being in a position that affords them extraordinary power; because they have more control, it's always at some level more their fault.

Whatever might go on in the imaginations of employees or the justifications of leaders, the fact is that those with the power to make decisions and to act will always have a disproportionate impact on working relationships, especially the relationships of those who come directly under their leadership. Great power, great responsibility. It is therefore important not only for leaders to consider their potential influence on working relationships broadly and continuity specifically, but for individuals to closely evaluate the character and quality of their relationships with leadership. After all, these are the people who are most likely to make or break your work experience. No matter how good your product is, how strong your customer base, or how stellar your performance—all factors you might base your confidence in your working relationships on—your continuity can be suddenly upended by a powerful individual. Bad leaders can become like bulls in china shops—a factor capable of creating intense havoc and irreparable damage if left unchecked.

Case Study: A broken promise

One way—perhaps the most powerful way—in which leaders can make or break continuity is through their promises. What sorts of promises a leader makes, to whom they make promises, and the faithfulness with which they keep promises have an indelible impact on the trust employees, customers, and every other mercantile or social entity within the ecosystem associate with the leader and their organization. In no small way, the working relationships we form to those we work with and the organizations for which we work are contingent on the promises those entities are willing to make and able to honor. Good leaders keep their promises. Bad leaders break their promises. In doing so, they invite disaster; not only do they damage the trust of their interlocutors, but their breach can reverberate through their businesses, undermining the resilience of the relationships that make their work possible.

I witnessed the power of a single broken promise firsthand in a college brewpub. Eight o'clock on a Friday morning, graduation weekend. The usually quiet college town was already starting to swarm with soon-to-be graduates, proud parents, stately faculty, and frantic event staff. For the brewpub, it was the busiest weekend of the year. Over the next Friday, Saturday, and Sunday, the brewery would earn nearly 10% of its annual income through food and drink sales, hosting receptions, and selling kegs to graduation parties. If everything went well, the money they would make in the next three days would be enough to float them through the slower summer season. I was there to observe a pressure test, to see how the brewery and restaurant operated at its busiest. I planned for a hectic day. I hoped to see something interesting. I didn't anticipate a meltdown before the first beer was poured.

On my way through the employee entrance, I was stopped by a porter insisting that I needed to stay outside. The head chef and the rest of the back-of-house staff were standing around the small loading dock, checking their phones or smoking. This immediately indicated that something was wrong. I asked the head chef what was up, but he was vague. We couldn't go inside right now, and he didn't know when we'd be allowed back in. He wouldn't say what exactly was keeping us out. Gas leak? Rats? A break-in? But he was visibly agitated. When I tried to press further, his sous chef told me to fuck off.

We stood outside for nearly an hour before a smug-looking man who looked to be in his thirties emerged from the building trailed by an older woman with a leather briefcase overflowing with papers. They were in turn followed by a middle-aged man holding a white plastic bucket, in which was a length of heavy-gauge chain. The head chef and the younger man exchanged a brief word, and then the trio got in a pickup truck and drove away. The head chef signaled that we were clear to enter the building. Whatever the issue was, it had finally been resolved.

The head brewer and the general manager arrived shortly after within minutes of each other, as I was still outside writing notes. The head brewer hadn't heard anything about the situation. He was confused, curious, and hungover. The GM was much better informed, and absolutely furious. When the head brewer asked what was happening, the GM snapped, "What the hell do you think? [Owner's name] didn't pay the rent. *Again.*"

I learned the rest of the story from kitchen gossip, one of the most useful and reliable sources of ethnographic data-slash-shit-talking. The smug-looking man was the brewpub's landlord's son. He and his entourage—an accountant and a superintendent—had chained and padlocked the doors early that morning because the brewery was over three months late on rent. The owner chalked the whole situation up to a miscommunication (the GM astutely questioned how this miscommunication could have persisted three months running). The landlord felt he was being deliberately fleeced. Wanting to be taken seriously, he seized the property. The hour-plus we spent outside instead of opening was the time the owner spent scrambling to reach a resolution with the landlord. The landlord only relented when the owner personally delivered a check for the overdue amount.

In the months that followed, the door-chaining incident had a significant impact on the perceived stability of the brewery. Not externally. The drama was over well before the first customer stepped through the door. Rather, the damage was internal. Despite efforts from upper management to keep the event on the "down-low," the story spread across morning and evening shifts like wildfire. How could it not? By the end of the day, everyone had heard some version of it. There were embellishments: that there had been a shouting match between the owner and landlord in the street in front of the brewpub (there hadn't). That the general manager had tendered his resignation in protest (he was walking the floor while a busser told me this). But beyond the pageantry and bullshit, employees had real and legitimate concerns. If the business couldn't pay its rent on time, were paychecks next? If cash was that tight, maybe the place would close for good.

These worries intensified for the more established employees. The head brewer openly worried about his job security, talking to the sous chef and bartenders about whether or not he should start looking for another job. In private, he pointed to the difference in revenue between the brewery and restaurant—calculated out on a bar napkin—convinced that, if push came to shove, the owner would outsource beer in order to keep the more profitable restaurant and bar. Later that month, when the company credit card bounced a payment for grain and hops, the brewer started seriously updating his resume, considering jumping industries to a more stable accounting job. The general manager did not resign, but he wasn't okay with the situation. He prided himself on being professional and conscientious. He wasn't like so many others in the service industry who were constantly trying to dodge bill collectors. The owner's broken promise had damaged his own reputation. So he made a promise of his own: If he ever had to deal with a similar situation again, he was gone.

The cost

The chaining of the brewpub's doors represented a critical break in the organization's perceived ability to maintain continuity in its working relationships. The brewpub owner had not only broken the trust of the landlord by not paying his rent, but that of his employees as well. Service industry employees are, as a rule, generally used to the ups and downs of their industry. High seasons and low seasons, living large in times of feast and scraping by in times of famine. That's just how it goes. The uncertainty affords a continuity of its own: Tuesday afternoons are always shit, but Friday evenings make up for it. But the prospect of waking up one morning and, through no fault of their own, suddenly being unemployed stretched their tolerance too far. The job was risky, but no job was too risky. If ownership was asleep at the wheel on the busiest weekend of the year, how could they be counted on? And if it could happen once, it could happen again. How could they feel secure? Negative attributes like "unreliable," "unsustainable," and "broke" started popping up more and more in back-of-house conversations and at off-site (not so) happy hours.

If it sounds like a bleak situation, it was. The brewpub carried that scar for a long time. Some employees moved on to other restaurants and breweries, and while they didn't cite the rent incident (hereafter, *rentcident*) in their resignation letters (not that servers usually produce those), kitchen gossip linked cause and effect for them. All-hands meetings and leadership meetings were tense for a while after. Every decision or comment the owner made was met with extra scrutiny. If it weren't for the beer, working and researching there would have really bummed me out.

The good news, though, is that working relationships—especially strong working relationships—can bounce back. Resilience isn't the avoidance of crisis. It's the ability to roll with that crisis without it turning into a disaster. The brewpub rolled with it. While the owner may have been less conscientious in paying his bills, he was not a stingy person. He was big-hearted and open with his time, advice, and resources. If you were having a bad day, he would sit down with you at the bar, pour you a beer, and hear you out. If you were struggling to find a place to live, he would use his connections to find you a reasonably priced apartment (not easy in a college town). He always showed up as the life of the annual holiday party. As one brewer put it, "Say what you will about him, he does give a shit about his people."

Bit by bit, the working relationships within the brewpub improved. Even though employees recognized that the ball could be dropped again, they didn't feel like it would. In any event, they weren't worried about it, at least not enough to find work elsewhere. They had trust that things would be better, that the company would endure, and that their careers would continue. As I'll discuss later, working relationships may be delicate, but they are durable. Our relationships to work, like our relationships to friends and family, can be mended, stitched back together when they tear apart. They aren't decided in an instant, but in an aggregate of moments. Nor are they ever finalized; working relationships are works indefinitely in progress.

Creating continuity

The rentcident illustrates the interplay of an active approach to creating continuity in a world of work that is always partially outside of our control. As I've noted, partial control is what makes achieving continuity so difficult. You can lose your mind considering all of the things beyond your power that still impact how you live and work. You can burn yourself out chasing all the threads that ultimately can't be pulled or adjusted. My Buddhist friends always advised "detachment." Southern moms let Jesus take the wheel. I've never been great at either of those. What *has* worked for me is some advice I got when I started at a marketing agency: Develop an internal locus of control. In practice, this meant focusing your energy on the things you can control, rather than letting your way of thinking and acting be dictated by the things you can't control (the external locus). Applying this ethos to continuity, I consider these questions to stave off madness.

Are you actively developing your own sense of continuity?

While colleagues, employers, and macro forces can strengthen—or undermine—your confidence in the durability of your working relationships, these passive inputs are outside your locus of control. It's important to take stock of what you are doing within your locus of control to build your faith that you will be okay, come what may. This can be a difficult task, especially in moments when so much feels outside our control. Focus on what you *can* control.

Taking an active role in your professional development can inject some agency into your sense of continuity. As I noted previously, skills can create a sense of continuity even in chaotic times. After salary increases and bonuses, skills are the most requested form of employer investment by employees. For some demographics (e.g., young well-to-do professionals or comfortable middle managers), skills even surpass raises when professional respondents are asked what would most improve their commitment to an employer or build their overall confidence. This is because skills, like money in your bank account, *are* ownable. Even if you lose your job or a company—or industry—tanks, you can still walk away with your skills. In a world increasingly driven by knowledge work, skills are what Marx called the means of production, the essential tools necessary to create value in the market. Skills empower because they are power.

Building skills is within your locus of control. If anyone tells you that old dogs can't learn new tricks, that's bullshit. You're never too old, too experienced, or too specialized to learn new things. Learning to learn isn't so much an ability—humans naturally learn things. Rather, it's the confidence to be shit at something for a while, and to chart a course to—and follow through on—being not-so-shit at it. Practice doesn't really make perfect, but through repetition and perseverance, we can and do get better.

As a graduate student, I would often become frustrated when I had semesters full of theory seminars with very little practical methodology. When I complained to my advisor, he suggested a different perspective: If I wanted to learn research methodologies, what was stopping me from studying independently? The point of graduate school wasn't to learn specific things, but to (1) experiment with tried-and-true techniques for how to get up to speed on something rapidly to figure out our ideal learning style, and (2) to build the confidence that we could get up to speed on something rapidly when the time came. In short, it really didn't matter what material we covered in seminars, because that material wasn't really the point. Learning how to learn was the point.

I can confidently say I have only found two occasions in which my command of theory has helped me in my career. Once, I wrote an article for a client on union relations and was able to accurately cite a number of very powerful theories. (They didn't end up using the article …) Another time, I was able to make small talk with an academic-leaning stakeholder to pass the time while we waited for others to log in to the Zoom call. However, I am very confident in my ability to learn new things. In client services, the capacity to rapidly download industry background, product offerings, competitor audits, and win-loss data—all the information that makes up the working context of a business—is invaluable. In the broader world of knowledge work, expertise is the currency of the realm. You need to know what you're talking about (even if you heard about career transition services only the day before).

I don't remember who told me this, but they rejected the idea that people didn't like to read. "It's not that people don't like to read. It's just that they haven't found something they like to read yet." You can apply that same philosophy to learning. Humans like to learn new things. We learn new things all the time. What's hard is learning things we don't care about, which we have to do all the time, especially in the working world. There are tons of experts more qualified than me to give advice on pedagogy (and this book isn't intended as a how-to guide), but if you're struggling to learn a new skill, consider this: How *do* you learn about things you do care about? What steps do you take? What are your preferred formats? How do you measure progress? Take those same steps, formats, and measures and abstract them. How could you apply those to learning about something less interesting? If watching videos is your jam, check out YouTube for tutorials on agile workflow planning. If you like to learn by talking to experts or enthusiasts, hop on Reddit or LinkedIn and strike up a conversation with someone knowledgeable about SPSS. The point is that you know you are capable of learning. You just need to develop a method that makes sense for you.

The joy of learning aside, it is important to note, from a practical point of view, that not all skills are equally valuable. Take it from me, I have a master's in religious studies that I've been able to professionally leverage exactly zero times. And not all skills maintain their value over time. Being able to program in Python or do pretty much anything with AI are far more in demand than a degree in liberal arts, if job postings are any barometer. But technical skills are only as relevant as the technology they serve. Once upon a time, being able to shoe a horse would have made a ye olde listicle of top skills. In the age of automobiles, farriers are few. Operating systems and programming languages become obsolete in time. Such is the way of the world. Technical skills are seldom a source of long-term continuity.

There are some skills that retain value despite the capriciousness of human innovation. These evergreen skills are consistently relevant to work despite the ups and downs of economies, the idiosyncrasies of industries, or the relentless waves of new and shiny technologies.[18] Evergreen skills are durable because they help navigate human relationships. The world of work is fundamentally human—humans doing work for other humans to achieve human goals. As long as humans are around to work, that work will remain human. While it's certainly possible to imagine a *Jetsons*-esque future in which work as we know it is fully automated (save for one lone worker pushing a button), I would argue that, given our industrious nature, we would invariably move on to some other form of work. Speculation aside, humans aren't going anywhere soon, giving human-centered skills durable value.

Communication is one such skill. (Communication majors, rejoice!) Complex and involved communication practices are one of the major qualities that distinguish humans from other animals. Conversing in diverse languages. Sharing oral histories around a campfire or watercooler. Recording our histories in hardcover tomes or 140-character snippets. It would be impossible to imagine humanity as we know it without the communication practices that define us. It

---

[18] I prefer the term evergreen skills as opposed to the hard skills/soft skills dichotomy, for one because hard and soft are loaded terms, two because it sets the skills hard and soft represent into an artificial opposition, and three because I like the imagery of trees.

would be equally impossible to carry out any sort of meaningful work.

In the world of work, communication skills create immediate value. Many Work Tech solutions base their value proposition around accelerating, extending, or consolidating internal and external communication. Communication platforms enjoyed increased significance during the COVID-19 pandemic when videoconferencing and contactless ordering apps made business possible for those maintaining social distance. Even as the pandemic subsided, remote and hybrid work modalities have continued to fuel the innovation and optimization of communication technology. Generative AI also promises to transform communication, automatically drafting cover letters and auto-completing emails.

These technologies have done much to make professional communication more accessible. Even so, there are use cases in which generative AI and similar assistive tools have yet to be practically implemented. Public speaking and live networking are two that immediately come to mind. The ability to effectively communicate in live, person-to-person situations is evergreen. Whether in a boardroom or over Zoom, being able to confidently, clearly, and concisely present information is critical. Even more so if that information is complex or boring. Many of us have had the displeasure of sitting through a text-heavy slide deck read verbatim by a monotone presenter. Hopefully, we've also experienced the opposite: a dynamic speaker presenting data and strategy with a vibrant, engaging flourish.

Likewise, there's no real substitute for in-person events. Between 2020 and 2022, I attended dozens of virtual conferences and hundreds of virtual happy hours, and similar professional/social get-togethers. I've yet to experience a virtual event that is a real replacement for the physical article. Even VR-mediated speaking events and classrooms pale in comparison to the tangibility of being there. Rather than falling out of practice following the pandemic, in-person events have taken on new significance, especially for professionals who work entirely remotely; in-person events become an invigorating break from everyday work patterns, an opportunity to put actual faces to names and profile pictures, and a chance to bond the old-fashioned way.

Effective communication is more challenging in a virtual or remote space. Many of the social cues we use to navigate social situations, including body language and peripheral sounds of understanding (a crowd murmuring with assent or the light chuckle of a joke landing), are either obscured or entirely hidden. The challenges of digital interaction make strong communication that much more essential of a skill. In a world of shaky connections, camera-off meetings, and "Bill, you're still muted," we need the ability to clearly and engagingly disseminate information more than ever.

Empathy is another evergreen skill. COVID-19 and the Great Resignation brought concepts like employee experience and compassionate leadership to the forefront of workplace discussions. Challenging toxic cultures, ensuring flexible work modalities, encouraging work-life balance, and other efforts to promote a healthy work environment were less nice-to-haves and more need-to-haves in a candidate's market. While some have taken advantage of the post-pandemic recession and employer's market to deprioritize improving employee experience, many people leaders are trying to find ways to improve work experience on a budget by focusing on what they can control.

Empathy is the ability to understand the feelings of another. As long as humans have feelings that they would like other humans to understand, empathy will be a valuable skill. The Japanese word for human is *ningen*, featuring the ideogram for person (人) and the ideogram for interval (間). A Japanese professor once told me that the meaning of humanity in Japanese is the interval between people, that we realize our humanity because of a separation between ourselves and another. That separation or interval, the attitudes, behaviors, and beliefs that make "me" distinct from "you" is what creates the human experience and necessitates interpersonal skills. The professor's explanation is probably apocryphal, but it's a useful story to illustrate a fundamental dynamic of human life: We don't fully understand each other. We *can't* fully understand each other, because there is always an interval between you and me. But we can still try to understand each other, and we can acknowledge and appreciate that effort. That's where empathy comes in.

Empathy is a skill you can develop through practice.[19] Some people are more naturally empathetic than others (just as some people are more naturally extroverted or authoritative than others), but anyone can build their ability to understand others. I do not believe that humans can ever really fully understand the experiences or emotions of another, no matter how close we are to that person. The interval always persists. But we can make more effort to listen and to hear what our interlocutors are saying. Being a good—or even great—listener is an evergreen skill. Having the patience to listen to someone is noticed. Taking the time to listen is appreciated. Training ourselves to listen first and act second makes us more considerate and careful, especially in delicate situations. Empathy slows down action without creating inaction, encouraging us to make the next best step for ourselves and those within our working relationships.

There are certainly other evergreen skills to consider, but that topic falls outside the scope of this book. Suffice to say that any skill that helps you better understand, connect to, and make sense of why humans do what they do and feel what they feel will help you immensely in what is still, and likely always will be, a fundamentally human world of work.

Are you making promises you can keep?

Promises create continuity—they are the assurance that things will remain consistent. Often, our ability to anticipate what will happen next in the workplace is based on our trust in what someone else has told us: *This quarter will be profitable. You are in line for a promotion. There are no layoffs planned.* As I illustrated, nothing undermines the continuity of a working relationship quite as profoundly as breaking a promise.

---

[19] For a deep and practical examination of empathy in the workplace, see Loren J. Sanders' Empathy Is Not a Weakness: And Other Stories from the Edge (2023).

Promises don't need to be spoken or written down for them to be meaningful. Take the story of the brewery's near-closure for example: The brewery owner never outright said to his employees that he would always pay the bills on time (although that stipulation was likely in his lease agreement). Yet, when he broke that promise to the landlord, he also broke that promise to his employees. The result was a serious blow to the perceived job security that rattled those the employer relied on to run his business. This example also shows that promises can be tangential—promises made between two individuals can have a halo effect on those who observe the promise being kept or broken.

Workplace promises are especially potent when the promise breaks the script. We anticipate that businesses will not abuse us, that promises in the employee handbook about fair conduct are a matter of course. (Breaking this sort of promise would also open up the employer to official censure or litigation, adding another layer of continuity.) However, if an employer promises something that is unexpected, that creates a bigger effect on the working relationship. Businesses are under no obligation to offer remote work, but if an employer promises employees that they will always permit and support remote work, that promise will have a greater impact than boilerplate promises because it goes above and beyond expectation. The cost of upping the ante, however, is that unexpected promises have a proportionally greater negative impact when broken.

Leaders sometimes fail to see the logic here. I've had CEOs tell me that their employees have no right to be upset that they are rolling back a fringe benefits plan or reversing a flexible work policy because they aren't guaranteed in employee contracts. These perks shouldn't be an expectation, and thus employers shouldn't be held accountable for taking a perk away in the same way that they would be for rolling back healthcare or reducing salaries. But that doesn't really wash. If you give a friend a gift, and then return to their house a week later and take the gift back, it would be unreasonable to expect the former recipient to still be pleased despite the loss because they were able to enjoy the gift for a week. It would be reasonable to expect that person would no longer want to be your friend. (And if you're reading this example and thinking it doesn't really apply because working relationships and personal relationships operate on different sets of rules, you should really read the next chapter on reciprocity. TL;DR: they don't.)

But sometimes employers can make a promise with every intention of keeping it, only for circumstances beyond their control to make honoring that promise impossible or disastrous to the overall well-being of the business. Take this promise made by a marketing agency during onboarding: We want this to be the last job you ever have. Their intention was to create such a positive employee experience and such a stable business that anyone who wanted to stay at the business (assuming performance expectations were met) would be able to stay and want to stay. To make good on this promise, they offered a range of perks and benefits that went above and beyond competitors and clients: four-day workweeks, unlimited PTO, remote work, flexible hours, a VR headset for socializing with colleagues, etc. This promise felt sustainable during a period of growth, and it was. However, when the agency encountered a prolonged recession, leadership was faced with a difficult choice: Choose between risking the overall viability of their business in order to honor their promise to employees, or break that promise and lay people off. They ultimately chose the latter.

It was not a great employee experience, certainly for those let go, but also for those who remained. There was suspicion, anxiety, and talk of double-dealing. Employees lost a great deal of confidence and trust in leadership. What happened to this being the last job those who were fired would ever have? That was a script-breaking promise, and it had been broken. The ramifications were commensurate.

But rather than get defensive, leadership — including the CEO — admitted that their former promise was unrealistic. They apologized, and though some employees continued to be distrustful, many appreciated the leadership's willingness to own their mistakes. Leadership also took steps to fix what they could and improve where they had control. They endeavored to act with more transparency, hosting weekly ask-me-anythings with the CEO and senior leadership, and sharing more details about business performance and prospects. Critically, they also forged a new promise: to create a world-class learning experience for employees. They took steps to make mentorship more accessible, especially for those less outgoing, by assigning every employee a steward with similar or complementary skills that could directly advise on their career progression. They also encouraged retrospectives on weekly sprints, and set aside time to present case studies of projects that went particularly well or particularly wrong. These measures didn't fully erase the broken promise, but they did begin the slow process of rebuilding trust by *showing* that this was a relationship that could become stronger.

Employers and leaders especially need to be mindful of the promises they make with their employees, whether those promises are explicit or tacit. In the same way that being a trustworthy partner to customers encourages the continuity of return business, being a trustworthy employer encourages the continuity of working relationships within your organization. For every promise you make to employees, consider these three questions:

Is the promise actionable?
That is, can you make good on the promise in ways that are tangible and relevant to your employees? Don't promise generous PTO if your production schedule or guilt culture makes taking PTO impossible.

Is the promise sustainable?
Honoring the promise once is great, but can you honor it a hundred times? Can you honor it for everyone? Can you honor it even if the economy takes a dive?

Is the promise meaningful?
Finally, if you are able to sustain the promise, does it matter? Is it the sort of promise any of your employees will actually care

about? If you want to make a difference in your employees' working relationships, make promises that are meaningful. At the same time, beware that the cost of breaking that promise will be proportionate to its meaning.

The faithful cultivation of a work promise is also the basis for the next elemental thread, the thread that is most consequential in maintaining the long-term viability of working relationships, especially working relationships between the worker and the people and institutions with which they work. In the next chapter, I look at the most fundamental and important work promise of all: reciprocity.

RECIPROCITY

By giving, receiving, and reciprocating in a balanced, mutually beneficial way, we perpetuate working relationships.

Reciprocal relationships

Reciprocity, the law of balanced mutual give and take, is the work promise that sustains our working relationships. If without continuity we would go mad with uncertainty, then without reciprocity there would be no point in maintaining a working relationship at all. Through the continual practice of giving, receiving, and reciprocating, we first weave our working relationships and perpetuate those relationships for as long as the cycle continues.

Working relationships are not transactional. Market relationships are transactional. In exchanging your money for a monitor at an electronics store, you have entered into a finite transactional relationship. The connection between you and the clerk (and their store) begins and ends when you trade your money for the good. While the store would certainly appreciate your return business, after the money and monitor have exchanged hands, there is no further obligation to continue the relationship. The loop has been closed. Even when making large purchases on a line of credit, there is a defined end to the relationship, if not in the near future, at least on paper. After 20 years and 240 monthly installments, I would be glad to never interact with my former mortgage holder ever again.

Working relationships *cannot* be transactional because they have no predetermined endpoint. In practice, we act as if working relationships will continue indefinitely. This mirrors our personal relationships: While we may be able to point back to the interaction that started our friendship, we do not imagine those relationships as having a specific end. We don't come to the end of our 100th get-together and say, "Well that was nice, but our contract has been fulfilled. So long!" When a personal relationship does end (as they inevitably do), it is typically due to unforeseen and unwelcome circumstances: a falling out, estrangement, death.

Relationships with employers are also prefaced on the infinite. When you get hired as a full-time permanent employee (we'll talk about contract work in a minute), an employer does not schedule your last day during the onboarding process. There isn't an assumption that you'll work for 90 days or a year or a decade and that will satisfy your contract (unless of course you are on a contract). Rather, your employment is imagined to be in perpetuity by both parties. Employers go out of their way to avoid churn, to develop employees, and to safeguard institutional memory. Ask any leader which key performance indicators are critical to their bottom line; retention is almost certainly one of them. Employees also operate as if their relationship with an employer will continue indefinitely. While lifelong employment is largely defunct, people still strive to put down roots and grow in a company. And even if an employee only plans to work a day job for a year or two while they finish their novel, it would be unwise to reveal that to their employer. A permanent hire is assumed to be just that: permanent.

Freelancers and other temporary employees who have demarcated contracts are a variation to this rule, not an exception. While their employment has a specified end date, temporary employees and their employers across industries tend to act as if the relationships can—and will—continue beyond the contracted term. There are practical reasons for this roleplay. Temporary work is driven by referrals, with strong relationships being the key to a steady stream of lucrative contracts. The freelancer might be a priority candidate if their position becomes permanent, or bring continuity to the team if they partner again on a later project. Freelance careers, like agencies, are reliably sustained by a healthy mix of repeat and new customers. It would be neither ideal nor sustainable to rely exclusively on one-off engagements.

Expectations frame and drive relationships. At the electronics store, the customer is expected to pay the sticker price and the clerk is expected to sell a product that is as-advertised and in good working order. In our personal relationships, expectations are much deeper and more nuanced. Learning the rules, the exceptions to the rules, and the exceptions to the exceptions is part of the game, both the fun and the challenge that we play every day. When compared, the expectations or rules that underwrite and animate an employer-employee relationship resemble our personal relationships far more than they do market transactions in terms of their number, complexity, and performance.

Social scientists love relationship rules. It really gets us going. There was a time when an anthropologist could sit on a log and watch villagers trade this or that or determine who sits where at a table and write a whole book about it. Much contemporary research falls pretty close to the relationship rules tree, building on the topic by adding additional nuances, exceptions, or case studies—this book included. Gift-giving practices are a particularly rich and storied area of study. This is likely because (a) gifts are observable and thus can be appraised and tracked by researchers, (b) every culture participates in some form of gift exchange practice, and (c) gifts are fun.

In his aptly named *The Gift*, written in 1925, sociologist Marcel Mauss identifies three rules or obligations that structure gifting rituals across cultures: the obligation to give, the obligation to receive, and the obligation to reciprocate. First, Mauss argues that people are obligated to give gifts if they want to create and sustain meaningful relationships with other people. If you want to declare your intention to enter into a relationship with someone or some organization, you must first give them something of monetary, ritual, or sentimental value. Bronislaw Malinowski, an early anthropologist and a guy who really loved rules, observed the pains that young men would go through to acquire special shell necklaces that they would gift to patrons in order to gain entry into the fraternal trading societies of the kula ring.[20] A more familiar example for many, offering someone a diamond ring signals your intent to spend the rest of your life together. Likewise, buying someone a cup of coffee is a classic and surefire way to strike up a friendship. If we want to start these relationships, or take them to the next level, we need to give.

Second, if someone is obligated to give, then someone else is obligated to receive. At least, they are obligated to receive the gift if they want to enter into that relationship. Accepting the gift signals that you are open to the connection. Refusing the gift closes the door. An engagement ring only achieves its purpose if the fiancée-to-be accepts it. Likewise, turning down the ring sends a powerful message not only about the quality of the ring, but the desirability of the relationship attached to it.

Giving and receiving a gift starts the loop of a relationship. These obligations are followed by a third: the obligation to reciprocate. Having received a gift, the recipient is expected to respond in kind by giving a gift of their own. Reciprocation begets further reciprocation: X gifts to Y, who gives to X, who gives again to Y. I get your coffee this week. You get my coffee next week. And then I'll get your coffee the week after. We flip-flop giving, receiving, and reciprocating week after week, so on and so on, into infinity. This continual gifting of coffees, Mauss argues, creates the justification for a relationship to continue indefinitely. Because you bought my coffee last time, we need to get together again so I can buy you a coffee. In reality, the coffee—and gifts in general—isn't really the point. Exchanging gifts just creates an excuse for us to keep getting together.

Giving gifts is different from exchanging money for goods in that, while shot through with obligations, gifts are *not* mandatory. There

---

[20] See Malinowski's Argonauts of the Western Pacific (1922), easily one of the most badass-titled books by an anthropologist. (See also A Diary in the Strict Sense of the Term, Malinowski's private diary that was published posthumously against his wishes, in which he complains about having to sit around all day and watch people trade stuff without being allowed to join in himself, because he of course did not have a necklace.)

is no law that says you need to reciprocate a gift. The obligation is a social convention, not a legal requirement. Because someone doesn't *have to give* a gift (even if we feel like they really *should*), the gift reads as a favor; it is something that goes above and beyond baseline requirements. Receiving a favor puts us at a disadvantage; someone has done something nice for us, so we *ought to* do something nice for them, at least if we want to keep that relationship. And if we do something above and beyond for someone else, they will likely feel they need to—and *want to*—reciprocate with a favor of their own. The constant back and forth, the *you got me last time, let me get you this time*, of reciprocation perpetuates the interaction.

Like transactional relationships, reciprocal relationships are driven by the exchange of valuable things—money, coffee, favors, etc. Unlike transactional relationships, however, reciprocal relationships don't keep meticulous track of the value being exchanged. Think about your relationships with friends or colleagues. You may know whose turn it is to buy coffee or the approximate value of the birthday gift you should reciprocate so you don't shame them for the gift they got you. However, most likely the calculus behind the exchange goes no deeper than "they got me last time, so I'll get them this time." *It's a deliberately inexact accounting.* It is unlikely that you have an exact figure on a little ledger book in your pocket, tracking inputs and outputs to ensure that you are square. Rather, we have a vague sense that our friend is indebted to us, and that we are likewise indebted to them, but the actual amount of that debt is never calculated and thus never paid in full. Paying off the debt would mean closing the loop, negating the impetus for the relationship to continue. The point is that you and I will continue buying each other coffee indefinitely, constantly in each other's debts, ensuring that there will always be a next time and, therefore, a relationship. The loop never closes.

Why do we go to all this trouble of giving, receiving, and reciprocating? The same reason humans engage in most optional behavior: because we like it. Being tied up with others in webs of obligation is enjoyable. It highlights our connections to other people.

It gives us a means to show we care, and a way to know that they care about us. Gift-giving gives us a sense of community. It gives our lives meaning. Not because of the gifts, but because of the relationships they activate, sustain, and enrich. We participate in the pageantry of gifts because we desire relationships and because we want those relationships to continue and grow. It would be a rare and supremely lonely individual who totally abstained from gift-giving; even Scrooge gave Bob Cratchit Christmas Day off prior to his haunting.

Now that we're several pages into this chapter on reciprocity, you may be wondering what all of this has to do with work. That's a fair question, and one I'll address shortly. The TL;DR: Working relationships are fundamentally and inescapably reciprocal. Employees and employers give, receive, and reciprocate to the same end of creating, affirming, and sustaining working relationships in perpetuity.

A note on balance

A note on the value of gifts: Gifts do not need to be exactly equivalent for their circulation to create a resilient relationship. In fact, differences in the perceived value of gifts is part of what makes the game of reciprocal exchange interesting.

Yes, you and your friend could go to the coffee shop every week and order the same medium-size black coffee. As long as you faithfully alternated every week, you would essentially be even in terms of money spent and value gained. However, in real relationships, it's more likely that your orders vary from week to week. Sometimes you pay for your friend's expensive mocha, and the next week they pay for your espresso. You lost out a little on that exchange. But maybe the week after that your friend treats you to a fancy seasonal frappe. Now the pendulum starts to swing back.

This accounting only really matters if you're comparing the amount spent on coffee over a finite period of time. Chances are, you're not. But that doesn't mean we don't have a tacit

---

sense of what is fair and balanced in an exchange. It would be incredibly awkward if we got our friend a $100 watch for their birthday and they reciprocated on our birthday with a new car. The relative values of a car and a watch are too different. Likewise, if our friend forgets their wallet week after week, we might become less inclined to keep going out for coffee with them. Just because we don't maintain a ledger doesn't mean we don't know when we are being taken advantage of.

Yet we can also play with this same sense of fairness to make a statement in our relationships. We can, for example, go above and beyond to mark an important occasion or to advance a relationship to the next level. We can surprise our spouse with a trip to Hawaii for our 10-year anniversary instead of going to our usual restaurant. We can buy our girlfriend a puppy to make things more official. We can also buy our friend coffee out of sequence because they've had a bad day, because money is tight this month, or just because.

We create rules and expectations around gift-giving to maintain healthy relationships, and then fiddle with those rules and expectations to enhance our relationships. These same practices of setting and defying gift-giving precedents also animate our working relationships. In fact, creating and breaking conventions takes on a significantly more competitive aspect in the war for talent and struggle for advancement.

Giving gifts at work

You may be feeling skeptical that professional relationships operate under the same rules of gift-giving and obligations to give, receive, and reciprocate as personal relationships. (If you read the previous note, you may be even more skeptical.) Your personal relationships are nothing like your relationships to your bosses and colleagues, you might be saying. Indeed, organizations insisting that their work cultures are a "family" has become a memetic red flag. Your skepticism is fair. After all, obligations in an employer-employee relationship do not seem vague, at least not at a professional company that has its shit together. Expectations are clearly spelled out in contracts and employee handbooks. There is clear communication. Chains of command. Workflows. Asana boards and kanbans. Transparency!

But on-the-record expectations are only part of the equation. In practice, working relationships are forged, maintained, and advanced through the same dynamics of giving, receiving, and reciprocating that weave our personal relationships. Employment might seem transactional. You exchange a certain amount of your labor to an employer in exchange for a certain amount of compensation. The salary, benefits, and other aspects of a total compensation package are based on a fair and/or competitive market valuation of the formal expectations the role and title entail. But beyond the employment contract is the labor that *exceeds* stated expectations. Have you ever been asked at work to go "above and beyond"? To give 110%? To dig deep? To put it all on the field? To take one for the team? These phrases convey more than a corporate love of sports idioms. They reveal a not-so-unspoken assumption on the part of leadership, of employees, and of business culture in general, that working relationships regularly entail giving discretionary effort.

Consider your own practice. Have you ever put in extra effort for a client? Have you ever worked late? Come in on your usual day off? Covered for a coworker? Took on projects over your typical capacity? Answered a question outside of your department? On how many of those occasions were you directly compensated for the extra labor you gave? Hopefully some, but probably not all. A related, but qualitatively different question: In how many of those instances did you *expect* to be compensated extra for your extra labor? Maybe some, but probably not all. Even so, you gave extra. Why? Let's face it: It was probably not out of the goodness of your heart. You may not have expected immediate compensation in the form of a bonus or gift card, but you did *anticipate something* for your extra effort. When we give more of ourselves than expected, we want to be recognized for that effort. If we bust ass to finish a project strong, we anticipate recognition. If we have a year of great quarters in a row, we anticipate a raise. If we add value to our company year after year, we anticipate a promotion.

We can anticipate these rewards. We can even strongly believe we deserve these rewards. But we cannot absolutely expect them in the same way we expect our salary or benefits. Unlike our job requirements or a baseline level of performance, our discretionary effort is a gift we give to our employer. Be it recognition, a raise, or a promotion, we reasonably hope for a gift in return.

Even though there aren't any formalized rules demanding it, the gifting of discretionary labor for reward is essential to the survival and success of businesses and organizations of all sizes and across industries. If you could sit in on and observe any business on any street in any city, you would see gifts being exchanged at all levels of the operation; leaders to subordinates, colleagues to colleagues, and sellers to customers. Employers fundamentally rely on gifts from their employees; sick days or parental leave would be impossible without employees volunteering to pick up an open shift or acquiescing to pick up a colleague's responsibilities. An office or warehouse full of individuals only willing to follow the absolute letter of their contracts would be disastrous. Productivity would plummet. Customer success would crash. Employees who are willing to give gifts of their discretionary effort are extremely valuable, not only because of the impact their gifts make on the bottom line, but because of the culture of reciprocation they encourage among coworkers and customers alike. Wise leaders recognize and reciprocate those gifts, perpetuating the relationship and retaining the employee.

Workplace gift-giving is key to professional advancement. "Hard work pays off" is a key tenet of the American work ethos, and it serves as a poignant reminder that striving above the minimum is not only virtuous but that virtue ought to be rewarded. This fact is especially important for employees looking to grow their careers. Most employment contracts do not have clauses that promise promotions and raises at set intervals and/or if certain performance goals are met. Rather, promotions and raises are discretionary efforts on the part of employers to recognize, reward, and retain valued employees. They are also a means for publicly demonstrating to other employees what kinds of discretionary effort leadership hopes to see, the sort of gifts they would really like to receive.

Reciprocating for fortune and glory

What makes a *good* gift? What is appropriate for employees to give? What is fair for employers to reciprocate? What kinds of gifts will perpetuate and grow a working relationship? What do both parties actually want, and what can each reasonably afford?

I am very candid with my employer about the reciprocal nature of our working relationship, and what I want to give and receive in that relationship: fortune and glory. So much so that I have it in my email signature. Fortune and glory are more than average. They are outcomes that exceed expectations. It's a fundamental promise to employers, colleagues, and clients: I will go beyond the baseline to create fortune and glory for you *and* for me. This promise is symbiotic. We share in fortune and glory for as long as our working relationship persists, but our relationship ends when fortune and glory turn one-sided.

The road to fortune and glory—or whatever it is that you want from your working relationships—is paved with gifts. The more-or-less balanced reciprocation of unexpected (but also *kind of* expected, vis-a-vis the obligations that underlie gift-giving) gifts facilitates a productive and prosperous working relationship between employees and employers. Resilient working relationships are held together by the substantiated belief that if I give to you, you will give to me, and that you will do so adequately, happily, and consistently.

The value of a gift is in the eye of the beholder. What is considered a gift is subjective. If an employee puts in extra hours on a project and their boss responds as if that were expected from the beginning, that boss obviously doesn't see the employee's contribution as a gift. The ambiguity of value is what makes gift-giving in working relationships fraught. If someone puts their all into a gift and it falls flat with the recipient, the relationship between the giver and the receiver becomes strained. If the dissonance continues, the relationship will probably snap. Ultimately, there is no foolproof way to determine whether something will be received and reciprocated as a gift. That is the risk you take as the giver. However, I can share some practical advice based on my research across industries and cultures of what I have seen consistently work. Consider it a gift guide of sorts.

What employers want

In a gift relationship—and working relationships are fundamentally gift relationships—employers want discretionary effort. They want to get more than they paid for, at least more than their overhead for salaries. Certainly, mission statements and organizational values often list wellness and community as goals, and I'm not too cynical yet to say that some businesses really do care about the well-being of their employees, but working relationships are ultimately practical. We enter into working relationships—and others enter into these relationships with us—because we want something out of it. Just as employees want something out of the relationship, so do employers. And when it comes to gifts, employers want to have their expectations exceeded.

I worked with one employee engagement vendor who was very blatant in how they defined an "engaged" employee versus a "disengaged" employee. Engaged employees did more than what was expected of them. Disengaged employees did the baseline. That's it. When advising their clients on which employees they should retain and which they should deprioritize or let go, this vendor did not mince words: Keep the employees who overperform. The disengaged employees were only disengaged in the sense that they fulfilled the letter of their contracts. Their advice to employees who felt they weren't being adequately recognized? Talk to your direct supervisor about how you can improve your performance so that you can earn more recognition.

This vendor's hard line is an extreme example and not one to which I'm particularly sympathetic. That said, employers do generally value employees who can be relied upon to go above and beyond in the quality and quantity of their work. Whether that's a fair standard is another question entirely. (But gift-giving isn't really about fairness …)

I'm not a stranger to the espoused virtues of only fulfilling your stated job responsibilities, maintaining strict working hours, and other strategies for approaching an employee-employer relationship more transactionally. This line of advice has become increasingly popular among millennial and Gen Z professionals discussing working life on platforms like Reddit and TikTok. I agree with it insofar as that is the kind of relationship you want to forge with an employer.

But what I also want to make clear is that a transactional relationship is not what most employers are looking for, and generally not the kind of relationship they value. They want discretionary effort. In practical terms, this means building your skills to deliver top-quality work, saying yes when others say no, and making the overall success of the company a priority, especially when the chips are down. It's a golden rule lifestyle: You do unto your company as you would have them do unto you. Good (and smart) employers faithfully reward that effort. But there's no guarantee that an employer will. That's the risk you take in trying to strike up a more-than-transactional relationship. It may not seem fair, but if you want to play the game, you have to burn the candle.

This isn't an ode to bootlickers. If you let employers walk all over you, you've missed the point of this chapter entirely. Rather, elevating your relationship with your employer from transactional to reciprocal cuts both ways: They come to anticipate more out of you, and you are entitled to anticipate more out of them. You cannot afford to be passive in setting and policing your standards. Instead of becoming complacent, employees should heavily scrutinize the health and value of their working relationships. Is the relationship still serving you? Is it making your life better? Is it going somewhere? If the answer to any of these questions is no, then you should address how to get things back on track with the other party. If the problem persists, cut and run. No different than a personal relationship. Work is just a marriage without a priest.

What employees want

If you are a leader who wants to cultivate resilient working relationships with your employees, the kinds of relationships that will add durable value to your organization, you have to reciprocate. The big question—and one numerous clients have paid to better understand—is what gifts employees actually want.

In the past three years, I've conducted nearly a dozen research studies in categories including learning and development, wellness, rewards and recognition, and employee experience, and for populations ranging from Australian C-suite executives to Canadian front-line retail workers. A common question across all of these projects: What makes employees feel the most valued?

The consistent answer?

You can probably guess: more money. Wage increases, bigger salaries, better bonuses. Large research firms, media, and social media polls have confirmed the same. It's not really surprising. Money, after all, is the main reason most of us work at all. Money is practical. Unlike commemorative plaques, you can do something with it. Money, unlike vacation days, stock options, or pizza parties, is versatile. You can use it to pay a bill, send a kid to college, or even throw a pizza party (probably with much better pizza). Money is also immediate, a liquid asset you can use right now. In a precarious world, the ability to respond rapidly (and in cash) is tangible peace of mind.

If you don't have more money to give right now, don't worry. Opportunity is consistently second place. Employees want support in growing in their careers, and they highly appreciate employers that provide that support. In a recent study I conducted, employees who received professional development support from their employers were significantly more likely to feel secure in their jobs, were more likely to feel their relationship with their employer was authentic, and, even if they were let go from their job, were more likely to boomerang and refer friends and colleagues to their former company. Affinity. Loyalty. Appreciation. A personal bond. Whatever you want to call it, reciprocating with professional development opportunities encourages it.

If you're reading this and have started panicking because you're worried that your employees are going to start demanding you pay for their college degrees, don't. Employees don't expect the moon. In fact, in the same aforementioned study, only 19% of Gen X, millennial, and Gen Z respondents felt that employers should cover tuition for a four-year degree. Employee wishlists are much more down-to-earth: The most sought-after forms of employer-provided professional development are mentorship, career coaching, and leadership training. Workers anticipate—and value—gifts of professional development at key moments: to accommodate role expansions, to reward stand-out performances, and preceding and following promotions.

But like giving a good birthday present or surprising your partner with the perfect vacation, good gifts require strategy. More and more, employees want quality professional development over quantity. While some employees appreciate large libraries of on-demand, asynchronous content for professional development, most clients I've worked with that deploy or create these platforms struggle with utilization. Most employees just don't use them regularly. At one enterprise company, 40% of employees never even clicked the onboarding link to set up an account. Contemporary employees want something different.

The most utilized and impactful professional development, at least according to eNPS scores and exit interviews, is personalized, relevant, and practical.

Personalized: Effective learning meets the learner where they're at. Years ago, that was something of a mic-drop statement. That statement has lost some impact as more and more learning leaders and learning and development creators advocate for learning that adapts to the current needs, background, and ambitions of the learner.

Personalization is somewhat vague in practice. Many learning platforms and apps, like their wellness or fitness cousins, determine user paths based on past experience and learning objectives (usually determined through a questionnaire during account creation or as part of a demo) and augment those paths based on performance through the curriculum.

Personalization can also be a product of working with a human coach, mentor, or facilitator who leverages their subject matter and teaching expertise to create a program for the learner. This tends to be expensive in practice and beyond the budget of many organizations.

Whatever your budget, a worthwhile learning strategy has to go some of the way at least to meet learners where they are at. The whole point of learning is to elevate. As Diversity, Equity, Inclusion, and Belonging (DEIB) initiatives have made increasingly clear, employees occupy diverse starting places. A rigid learning strategy will fail to connect with and elevate all of your learners, undermining your mission and shooting your return on investment in the foot.

Relevant: If the professional development you're offering isn't relevant to your employees, why should they care? If a gift isn't useful or appreciated, it won't do anything for a relationship.

I worked with a brewery once that had an annual holiday party where they did a gift exchange. The head chef regularly brought the worst gifts: a used basketball, a tire puncture repair kit, a pair of cheap squirt guns. Employees joked that he probably picked them up from a gas station on his way to the party. Nobody really liked the chef, and his thoughtlessness during the gift exchange was regularly brought up as proof of how he "didn't give a shit."

Is the professional development you're offering actually relevant to your employees? Is it a gift they can use? Will it help them succeed in your organization? Would it help them succeed at another organization? A strong strategy answers yes to all of those questions. If the only new skills you're teaching are how to use systems or tools proprietary to your company, that's not really hitting the mark. If you're worried that empowering your employees with relevant skills will enable them to find employment elsewhere, then you should build the quality of your working relationships—with reciprocity, for example. Holding out on reciprocity will only continue pushing them toward the door.

Practical: Learning worth reciprocating is practical—i.e., you can use it. Have you ever received a gift and wondered, "What am I going to do with this?" Good gifts are useful. They enable you to do something you couldn't do before—a tool that helps you finish a home project, a good book that passes an evening, a stylish rug that ties the room together.

Did you ever sit in high school and wonder, "When am I ever going to use this?" That pain point never really goes away. Professional learners encounter that question all the time. This is why online certificate programs justify their cost of entry with lists of the potential applications of the skills you'll learn and testimonials of past students who got their dream job. See? This is useful. This will get you to where you want to go.

Marketable skills—skills that people will actually pay you (more) for—are practical. It's also what many employees want out of professional learning, and what they most appreciate receiving from an employer. (We looked at this in greater detail in the previous chapter.) Mentorship is also highly valuable when that relationship provides valuable experience and connections. Like career coaching, effective mentorship can also help employees chart a course to their ideal career, and establish the "so what's" that drive them to show up and stay invested. More on purpose in the next chapter.

Gift strategies

Reciprocal relationships are driven by a strong gift-giving practice between employers and employees. The most meaningful gift employees can offer is discretionary effort—going above and beyond when and where it counts. The best way employers can reciprocate this effort is with gifts that are personalized, relevant, and practical. If you want to create resilient working relationships with or in your organization, you need to have a strategy for creating and distributing the gifts that will spark and feed these relationships. Whether you are an employee looking to build your career or an employer trying to improve retention, consider these questions when creating and validating your strategy:

Is it a good gift?
Is the gift desirable to the other party? Is it useful? Is it personalized? Is it relevant to their needs and interests? Is it practical to those needs and interests?

Is giving the gift sustainable?
Can you give the gift over and over again without burning through your resources or burning out yourself? Is it something you actually want to give? Don't set a precedent of giving gifts you either can't or don't want to afford.

Does the gift represent you?
Gifts are all about personal relationships. The gifts we give should

represent the people in the relationship. Not just the recipient, but the giver too. Does the gift communicate something about you to the receiver? Does it say something about what you value? About what you believe?

If you answered no to any of these questions, you have options. You can make a gift better suited for your target audience. Alternatively, you can find a recipient who is a better fit for the gifts you have. You have a limited amount of time, resources, and capacity to give gifts. Whether an individual or an organization, no one has an endless capacity to reciprocate. Pick your partners mindfully. Give and receive where and when it makes sense. And cut your losses when reciprocation stalls.

When reciprocity unravels

Whatever shape your practice of gift-giving takes, it's essential to be mindful of the gifts you give, receive, and reciprocate. Even with the best of intentions, reciprocity can go off the rails. Gifts are incredibly powerful, setting working relationships into motion and keeping them in motion. But that power is double-edged: Gifts—even gifts that initially seem like great ideas—can also create unintended consequences that erode the resilience of working relationships. Again, with great power comes great responsibility. It was true for Spider-Man, and it's true here.

In my research on workplace gift-giving, a lack of mindfulness was most dramatically—and at times tragically—illustrated by the craft brewing industry's ubiquitous practice of supplementing compensation by paying brewers in beer. The following is one brewer's story, but one representative of many I encountered over five years of ethnographic research in the American and Japanese craft brewing industries.`

Case Study: The wolf at the door

Ryan liked being a brewer, but he had grown to hate craft beer culture. "I think I was kind of like everyone when I first started," he said, sipping a mug of coffee and looking over some paperwork in his small downtown brewpub. "I was like, oh, I get to make beer and drink beer while doing it, that's sick!" In the beginning, it had been pretty sick.

Ryan was the only brewhouse employee. Neither of the two owners had brewing experience, and the small establishment couldn't support an assistant. He was largely autonomous, with very little oversight. As long as he kept the beer flowing, no one worried much about how he was doing it. Ryan, a former chain pizza employee who was used to being needled by a host of supervisors, took advantage of his newfound freedom and the near-limitless supply of beer.

Ryan started most mornings with a beer straight off a fermentation tank. To "switch gears" for a day of brewery work, as he put it. He'd often drink throughout the day, passing the time while a kettle boiled or a keg was cleaned with a pint or two. He often hosted his non-brewer friends on slow days. "It must be great to hang out and drink all day," his friends said. It was. "I hung out after work for a couple of beers with the other managers almost every day," Ryan recalled. "Sometimes I would pick up a shift at the bar so I could make a little extra cash. Then I would hang out and drink with the bartenders as they got off their shifts." His brewpub had a liquor license, and his employers were equally open-handed with spirits. "I was obliterated most nights and hungover the next morning. Then I'd drink a bit to take the edge off, and around we'd go again."

"It obviously became a problem," said Ryan. He started tripping over hoses in the brewhouse and hitting his head on opened manway doors. "My coordination got really bad. It became a running joke with the kitchen and waitstaff." Then he started to forget things. "I'd misplace tools or forget what step of a recipe I was on. Thank god I never messed up a beer too bad, but we definitely had some interesting beers when I'd forget which hops to use. It got really bad for a while," Ryan recalled, "I was totally out of control."

Then he got a wake-up call. "Yeah, one of the oldest breweries in the state shut down. I heard from my buddy that the brewery got a yeast infection, but the head brewer was too drunk or high to fix it." Leadership eventually fired the head brewer, but the damage to the brewery's reputation and profits was too severe. "I wasn't that far gone," Ryan noted, "but I was definitely on track." He didn't want to create the same "shitshow" that the other brewer had, to become "a joke" in the community, as he put it.

I asked if he stopped drinking. "No," Ryan laughed. "I'm a brewer. How would that work?" Instead, Ryan cut back, creating a set of rules to reign in his drinking. "I don't drink before noon, that's one. I also don't drink at the brewery if I'm going out with friends later. And I only have one drink every three hours or so." The rules helped. "I'm not tripping and forgetting stuff as much. I also don't feel awful all the time."

But Ryan's self-imposed intervention came at a cost. For an industry that prides itself on creativity, Ryan sighed, the craft beer community was awfully conformist. "I honestly don't feel like I experienced peer pressure until I became a brewer." Ryan recalled how early in his career he had worn a suit to a local brewery event. "It wasn't a tuxedo, just business casual." The other brewers, dressed in plaid shirts and trucker hats, mocked him the entire evening. Years later, conference and festival attendees would still ask him where his suit was. But the questions about drinking were the worst, he noted. "Every time I go out for dinner or to someone's brewery or they come here, if I don't drink or I only have one beer, it's like, 'What's wrong? Don't you like beer anymore? You need to relax, man.'"

Ryan worried he had developed a reputation in the brewing community for being uptight. Other brewers probably thought he was boring, or a prude. He had also grown tired of the same jokes: friends pretending they forgot he was a brewer or asking him if he had to hire an assistant to sample his beer. "Whatever," he shrugged. "I don't even like hanging out with brewers anymore."

Ryan's experience underscores the significant social pressure within the professional brewing community to drink, and not only to drink but to maintain a relaxed and open attitude toward the overconsumption of alcohol. In a society where regular and sustained drinking is considered both the normative behavior and the avenue through which meaningful relationships are formed and maintained, abstinence is both deviant and the grounds for social exclusion.[21]

Ryan's experience is not unique. Nor was his consumption of (and access to) alcohol entirely his own doing. While social expectations certainly play a significant role in pressuring brewers to drink and drink often, the incentive to (over)consume beer is built into the job itself. One of the most common benefits listed on brewery job postings for any level position is free beer. Indeed, for many breweries, especially new startups or small operations with few employees, a supply of beer on the house may be one of the only benefits the brewery can offer. In an industry where unpaid internships are still relatively common, beer can be the only form of compensation. Many brewers I spoke with recalled being exclusively "paid in beer" early in their careers, walking out of the brewery with a six-pack or growler at the end of an eight- or 10-hour shift. But even for part-time or full-time paid employees, beer still represents a significant portion of their total earnings. "When I started, I was getting paid $30,000 a year full time," said Ryan. "At least I had free beer."

In this paradigm, drinking beer is a way of realizing the value of one's labor. You may be paid $15/hour as an assistant brewer, but if you drink three pints at $7 each during or after your shift, you've effectively raised your hourly rate to over $17. If you don't drink, that value is lost. The pressure to realize one's value through beer is even more pronounced in businesses that control beer consumption through

---

[21] In his 2015 deep dive into Japanese drinking culture, Paul Christensen argues that drinking maintains both notions of masculinity and feelings of belonging in Japanese white-collar professional society. It is because of this double pressure that public and professional alcohol over-consumption is so pervasive in Japan (if you've ever walked down a street in Tokyo and seen a man in a suit sleeping on a park bench or in a hedge, you know what I'm talking about), and why alcoholism is such a tricky problem to tackle for those afraid of damaging their social and professional relationships.

weekly or monthly "beer rations" or daily "shift beers." One part-time keg washer I spoke with worked at a brewery where employees were allowed to take any defective or expired beer cans from a pallet at the end of their Friday shifts. The employee complained about needing to buy a second refrigerator for his garage to store the beer he was taking weekly. When I suggested that he just not take more beer, he scoffed. "It's use it or lose it, man. I'm not going to say no to free beer."

Mindful reciprocity

We rely on reciprocity to drive working relationships. We do so even when we don't realize that's what we're doing. This is why being mindful of our working relationships—what forms, sustains, and grows them—and having a strategy to frame and guide aspects of those working relationships' reciprocity is so important. It's also why regularly reevaluating your strategy—what kinds of discretionary effort you give as well as the particulars of your organization's compensation package—is essential. The particular qualities, costs, and potential impacts of the gifts we circulate are critical, but also volatile. What cultivated a healthy relationship today may undermine it tomorrow. What may have met a recipient's needs at one stage in their career or their life may not help them reach the next.

If gifts can make or unmake resilient working relationships, we need to closely consider how we create, circulate, and appreciate those gifts. And when we understand our working relationships as not transactional, but reciprocal—a constant flow of gifts—we are better able to navigate our world of work and forge the kinds and qualities of relationships when and with whom we need and want. Whether you are an individual contributor or a leader, consider the kinds of gifts you give and receive. In this context, consider the questions I posed earlier, with a small, but not insignificant, addendum to the last:

Is it a good gift?
Is giving the gift sustainable?
Does the gift represent the kind of working relationships you want to create?

PURPOSE

Purpose is the belief and validation that your work is meaningful to you and those important to you.

Rise and grind

My phone alarm chimes, pitiless, as I roll off my futon onto the hard laminate of a studio flat; 5:30 a.m., another early Thursday morning in Okinawa. It's only halfway through the workweek, but my back already aches from hoisting 20-liter milk jugs, my legs are stiff from long hours on a cement floor, and my hands are burned, cut, and stained orange. Too tired for shoes, I don a pair of flip-flops—I'll have the energy for work boots later—splash some water on my face, grab my keys, and stumble through the heavy metal door into the cool twilight. A short drive, then a stop at the little convenience store at the intersection of the country road leading to the workshop. I stare at the little self-service coffee maker as it prepares an iced coffee, whirring and bubbling, one of the few uncomplicated pleasures in my working/ research life. An hour later, the milk is pasteurizing, and Ellen is taking a silent inventory. It's rare for her to say much before lunch. Prepare the ice bath, add the culture, set with culture. A garlic cheddar again; I'll have to scrub my hands raw if Lauren wants to go out tonight. At lunch, I scroll through Facebook. Friends and colleagues on summer holiday, air-conditioned libraries, coffee shops in Tokyo, one guy's taking the month to sail and "really reconnect." I put my phone away because I'm worried I'm becoming too negative, too jaded, but then I take it out again to upload a photo of yesterday's pecorino. Back at it, the cheese is ready to be cut, strained, cubed, and cheddared. My cheddaring doesn't look as nice as Ellen's, and it bothers me (I take a picture of her basket to study later at home). Cut again, hand-toss in garlic powder—I should just buy gloves—press, and watch Ellen try to Tetris the new cheeses into an already-cramped fridge. I clean the floors while Ellen finishes some paperwork. Taking out the trash, I pause to say hello to one of the barn cats sleeping in a moldy cupboard. It ignores me, but the small one-sided interaction picks me up a little. Ellen steps outside, locking up. "See you tomorrow then?" We chat a little about Friday's plan while we walk to our cars. I check Instagram later that night; my uncle comments, "It looks like you're having fun! (cheese emoji)." I think about the new chili pecorino Ellen's okayed for tomorrow, my first approved recipe. A small light in an otherwise weary world. I "like" my uncle's comment, set my alarm, and crash into sleep.

When I look back at my field notes from the year I spent working in artisan shops in Okinawa, I'm struck by how weary I was. How ground down I felt. How little fun seemed to factor into it. Sure, there were moments of excitement here and there—a hurricane that made the cheese shop flood, big community festivals, grand openings and soft launches—but the average day was: Get up, go to work, make something, interview someone, go home, write notes, go to sleep, repeat. Week after week, month after month. I sometimes wonder how I stuck it out. Nobody was forcing me to be there. I could have done my research about anything. The research university that was sponsoring me only had a vague idea of what I was doing, and seemed to be satisfied with that level of detail. Sure, I wasn't suffering in a real sense, but I also wasn't thriving. I wasn't stimulated. Like so many people at multiple points in their lives and careers, I was just kind of grinding along.

In those moments, and in reflecting on those moments, I've asked myself and others the same question over and over again: Why? What is the point? What makes you get out of bed in the morning and keep going? Some have made the sort of impassioned speeches you see on cable television shows where CEOs sneak around in wigs and feign interest in working-class hardships. Some have offered genuinely inspiring reflections. Some have just told me to fuck off. Most, however—including myself at many points in my research and career—just don't have a clear answer. It's not that they don't know. It's rather that it's difficult to articulate.

This chapter attempts to articulate the purpose behind why we work and how our purpose shapes and is shaped by our working relationships.

Finding purpose

Purpose is a difficult subject to tackle, be it related to work generally or daily life broadly. In part, this is because purpose is fundamentally subjective: What is meaningful and impactful to someone is as varied as the person answering it. It is also because purpose is so nebulous: It can change rapidly without warning. Add to this that most of those I worked with during my research had neither the time nor the patience to explore the subject. Not because it was out of their depth—many artisans, and brewers especially, have the souls of warrior poets and minds of philosophers. Rather, it was too romantic or too existential to discuss in the flow of work when one's attention needed to be focused on the minutiae of detail. As one colleague regularly put it, getting too deep in the weeds about purpose was "academic bullshit" that could wait until after the brew day.

Even so, the concept would pop up organically from time to time in different contexts. Sometimes interlocutors used purpose as a synonym for their reasoning behind a decision, their "purpose for" doing a project, starting a business, or contributing to a community. Others used purpose as *raison d'etre*, their reason for being. In Japan, artisans would talk about their *ikigai* (生き甲斐), a phrase that also translates to reason for being and combines the ideograms for "life" and "worth." Western craftspeople tended to use purpose and passion interchangeably in articulating their drive or determination to endure.

Executives and designers I've worked with in the Work Tech market usually point to their mission, vision, and values as the company-vetted purpose behind a product or service.

The common thread connecting these interactions: a drive forward, the impetus to stay with and continue their work. It was the inaudible, nagging voice in the back of their heads that, despite pain, frustration, and monotony, motivated brewers, warehouse workers, and directors of human resources to persistently get out of bed and fill their boots. It was the answer to why: Why do this, why stick with it, why keep getting out of bed? Because [insert purpose here].

Work has purpose when the worker believes their work makes a meaningful impact *and* has that belief validated. *A purposeful* impact is meaningful. The meaning behind that impact can be anything. Think about your own work—what gives it meaning? Who does it affect, and in what ways? Maybe it provides for your family. Maybe you believe it supports your organization or your community. Maybe it makes the world of work a better place. Maybe it's revolutionizing your industry. Maybe your work is just interesting, challenging, and enjoyable. It doesn't really matter. As long as you believe that your work has a meaningful impact, you're halfway there.

Validation is the other half. Generally speaking, we can only sustain our belief in the impact of our work—and thus the feeling that our work has purpose—if that belief is validated in some way. Your belief that your work provides for your family is validated when you can pay your bills or go on a family vacation. Your belief that your work supports your organization is validated when a supervisor acknowledges your contribution or gives you a raise. Your revolutionary ambitions are validated when shareholders line up to invest money in your idea. Your enjoyment in work is validated when doing it actually releases endorphins.

Without validation, maintaining a sense of purpose in our working relationships is unsustainable. Consider Santa Claus. A child's belief in Santa Claus fades when enough empirical and anecdotal evidence stacks up to suggest their belief is unfounded. Other kids at school saying it's just your parents. Not getting the puppy you asked for in your letter. The fact that your house doesn't have a chimney. An 11-year-old staying up all night and not hearing—or seeing—a thing. So, too, does our sense of purpose fade when our belief in the impact of our work isn't validated. It's difficult to convince yourself that your job is worth it if you can't make ends meet after working 40 hours a week, or that your work is making a difference if your boss never congratulates you after a big presentation. No one, save for the most die-hard zealots, is able to persist in an activity without their faith being rewarded at least occasionally.

Burning hot

Purpose is the slow, steady, subconscious flame sustaining workers through the everyday grind. As a fire, purpose must be constantly fed. As a relationship to work, to an organization, and to an industry, it takes two to keep the fire burning. Workers burn hot when they see their efforts rewarded: praise and recognition, professional development opportunities, a promotion, a raise. Purpose is also internally rewarded: the satisfaction of overcoming a challenge, of surviving a crunch period, of doing work that was intellectually or creatively rewarding. When properly fed, the flame of purpose grows exponentially. Like a wildfire, it can rapidly spread to others in an organization, setting them ablaze.

Yet all fires run the risk of burning low. Purpose is a tricky thing—like a flame, it's volatile. Purpose is vulnerable. Organizations change, interests dim, routines can yield diminishing returns. Burnout has become the boogeyman of human resources, and for good reason. When top performers disengage, the whole organization suffers. Burnout is contagious, gradually, inexorably dissipating the heat of a workforce. And for those who experience it, burning out is often a slow and painful process, a death by a thousand cuts.

Case Study: Burning low, burning out

I first met West during the earliest stages of my fieldwork, when I was still bumming around small-town brewing communities to see who might be willing to host a Ph.D. student with no practical industry experience. He invited me up to his brewery for a tour and a chat. West was nearly six years into his career, not quite a veteran, but seasoned and confident in his practice. He was intelligent, witty, and charismatic. Pointing out various pieces of equipment and explaining their functions, he described the *work* of brewing; it wasn't a hobby, you couldn't "mess around," or do anything by half-measures. But that didn't mean the job wasn't fun. "You get to make beer for a living," he laughed. "How many people get to do that?" He saw himself as a brewer for his community; if the people sitting at the bar were happy, he had done his job. After leaving West, I jotted down my impression in a notebook: "diligent" and "easygoing."

We connected again the following winter, this time for an in-depth job shadowing. West was only a year older, but it hadn't been an easy year. Working in greater proximity, it quickly became apparent that West was deeply frustrated with his situation. Beer sales were considerably slower than previous years. Before, West recalled, the brewery would go through 30 kegs on a Thursday. Now it was barely kicking 10. The general manager blamed liquor sales for cannibalizing beer sales, but the brewer couldn't help but wonder if there was something he was doing wrong. "Maybe people just aren't drinking beer these days," he occasionally suggested, as if to drive away his lingering anxieties. Poor sales were coupled with a seemingly endless list of broken or malfunctioning equipment: A failing boiler, holes in the stainless-steel kettle, and leaky pipes were just some of the issues that kept West up at night. There wasn't money to fix anything, however. The brewery owner had recently acquired a new venture that was sucking up most of the available capital. It was starting to feel like the brewery was no longer a priority.

Despite the setbacks, West remained cautiously optimistic; though things were currently in a rut, they would get better. He expressed confidence in his own energy and ability to shake things up. Assuming that drinking behaviors were cyclical, West believed that customers would inevitably turn back around to beer. West planned to develop some new recipes and fine-tune some old ones. He also toyed with the idea of cultivating a hop garden on the roof. When drinking beer became trendy again, he would be ready.

The following summer was particularly cruel. Not only did sales continue to slow and ultimately stagnate, but August saw the departure of West's longtime co-head brewer. After much deliberation and a great deal of anxiety, West's partner left the brewery to pursue an exciting independent position where he would have full creative control. Though West characterized it as a "stupid move," wondering aloud often and to anyone who would listen why someone would leave such a "cushy" job, I got the feeling that this incredulity served to mask a sense of jealousy: His partner was leaving for bigger and better things, excited to finally brew all the weird stuff he wanted to try, while West would be left behind in a crumbling brewhouse, still stuck in a rut, but now a degree lonelier. This drama distracted from any significant innovations. The hop garden never materialized. Toward the end of that summer, West first suggested, quite out of the blue, that perhaps this life was no longer for him. "Sometimes I just want to walk away."

I left after the summer to conduct fieldwork, but kept occasional tabs on my friend. From a long distance, things seemed to be incrementally improving. He had hired a new assistant with no experience, someone he could train from the ground up. Showing him the ropes seemed to give West a new purpose. But things soon began to deteriorate. The assistant was not a quick learner, and didn't seem eager to study. He was also sensitive to criticism, and became surly in the face of reproach. West was frustrated. He'd occasionally vent his frustrations in an email or text, wondering whether he should just fire the assistant. Maybe he would be better off just working alone?

Despite the turbulent working relationship, the business year was relatively healthy, and the brewery saw a slight uptick in production and revenue. Maybe the wheel was finally starting to turn. Increased profits made it possible for West to attend the Craft Brewers Conference for the first time in years. It was an inspirational experience; West returned excited to try some trendy new styles and techniques that he hoped would capitalize on the brewery's recent momentum. I was back from Okinawa at this point, working at another brewery while writing, but I would visit occasionally to catch up. From time to time, I would see flashes of West's old fire: brainstorming ideas, networking with local businesses and nonprofits, participating in collaborations. It was reassuring to see him work to pull himself out of a slump.

However, the conference seemed to be a high point from which West's enthusiasm began a perpetual descent. Over the next year, he took hit after hit. The first blow came almost immediately after he returned from the conference. In his absence, his assistant had committed a series of critical mistakes that left West no choice but to fire him. It was an ugly breakup, with the assistant accusing West behind closed doors of neglecting his training and failing to properly utilize his skills. By all accounts, the assistant was neither skilled nor eager to work. This upset West all the same, who took the unwarranted criticism very personally. This was followed by West winning a gold medal in a statewide competition for a new recipe. West was exuberant, texting me late Friday evening to share his victory. But after the brewery ownership failed to acknowledge the achievement, he became proportionately bitter. In the past, West explained, his success in competitions had been met with praise, social media boasting, and even bonuses. This time, the general manager gave a half-hearted "cool." The owner forgot to respond to the text. "See," West worried over a beer, "they don't even care ..."

West took a chance with his next beer, a beer featuring Sorachi Ace, a Japanese hop varietal with a unique aroma and flavor profile that can either tend to intense lemon or dill. West had never used Sorachi Ace, rarely tasted it, and was unsure exactly how to control for lemon and avoid dill. Yet he took the risk, and almost immediately regretted it. I spoke with him the day after he brewed it: He was convinced it smelled of dill. Pacing the brewhouse, he repeated, "This was a mistake." And while the beer turned out well—and very lemony—it sold slowly. Wanting to strike gold again, he considered repeating the competition beer, but realized that he had neglected to write down the recipe's specific ratios. It was around this time that I noted West a heavy drinker from the time I had first known him—had significantly increased his alcohol consumption.

As the year wore on, West complained regularly about needing a vacation. "I just need to get away from this place," he grumbled. "It's killing me." But after West returned from a weeklong cruise, his apathy quickly set in again. He'd spend long hours sitting at the bar, drinking beers (and the occasional glass of wine) and playing on his phone, joking with the bartenders about how little he planned on accomplishing that day. He moaned almost daily about being bored. But if someone suggested a new project, he'd generally dismiss the notion. West wanted a raise—he hadn't received one in over three years—and why should he take on extra responsibilities without additional compensation? After all, it wasn't his fault that work was slow. West fell back on the claim that people just weren't buying beer, ignoring that his former partner and several other colleagues were in the midst of expanding their operations to meet growing consumer demand. But I don't think the discrepancy was lost on him. Rather, his lack of productivity gradually eroded his drive and self-worth. I asked him during a visit what he planned to do that day. "I don't know," was his reply, "maybe jump off the roof." A joke, but a telling one.

When I left West, he was miserable. His body ached, especially his back and around his kidneys. He spoke of having no energy, no ambition. He openly talked about quitting his job to bartenders, managers, and anyone else who would listen. He couldn't quit, however, because he needed the salary and benefits, and what other job would offer him the flexibility to leave when wanted and drink for free when he stayed? He darkly referred to himself more than once as a "professional alcoholic." But in moments of clarity, West glimpsed himself through the jokes and bravado. As he worked through his sixth pint of the afternoon, he lamented, "I'm just burned out, man. I'm just burned out."

The employer's dilemma

Some may be reading this and thinking that the brewer's employer should have acted to prevent his burnout. Working with clients dealing in employee engagement and experience solutions, and with business leaders trying to improve key performance indicators like retention and engagement through experience initiatives, I've likely seen all of the tricks: more recognition, better development opportunities, points-based swag stores, wellness apps. The list goes on. While these can all be great strategies for validating the meaning of an employee's work, they do not and cannot represent a substitute for that employee's purpose.

These are some uncomfortable truths about purpose:

1. **Employers can't cultivate purpose.**

   While employers take point on ensuring continuity and share in sustaining relationships through reciprocity, they have very little input into an employee's purpose beyond validating it. They can feed the fire, but they can't start it.

2. **Employees must supply their own purpose.**

   The world of work is BYOP. Your employer can tell you how you should work, where you should work, when you should work, with whom you should work, and what you should work on. They cannot tell you why you should work. That needs to come from within. If you don't know why you work, you need to do some soul searching.

3. **Employers who think they can provide a relevant purpose to their employees have delusions of grandeur.**

   My advisor told me once that he was confident that he could give me a thesis, sketch out a set of research questions, and send me to a field site, and that I could come back in 18 months with a complete dissertation project. However, that wouldn't be my dissertation. It would be his. Even if I did all the work, the impetus behind the project wouldn't be my own. I wouldn't really own the project, wouldn't really be passionate about the project, and wouldn't really feel motivated to continue the project if the driving idea behind it wasn't my own. That's why I was to "fuck off and figure it out" myself.

4. **Missions, visions, and values cannot give employees purpose.**

   Related to the above, purpose has to be something employees develop on their own. Organizational mission statements and catchy values can get employees thinking. They can provide employees with the words or concepts to parse and articulate their own attitudes, behaviors, and beliefs. They can tell employees what their company expects. They can also show employees how to execute on those expectations. They cannot fill in the blank of why your employees work. That's their job, not yours.

5. **There is no such thing as a bad purpose.**

   Your purpose is your own. Whatever it is, roll with it. If your purpose is to make a shit-ton of money, great. If your purpose is to save the whales, awesome. If your purpose is to impress your friends, that's fine. Nobody cares, and if they say they do, they shouldn't. Nobody can tell you your purpose, and nobody can judge your purpose, either. Everyone's purpose is unique to them, and because everyone is equally unique, all purposes are equally worthless to anyone but the purpose holder.

6. **If you feel that your purpose exactly aligns with your organization's stated mission and values, and you are not one of the founders, you need to dig deeper.**

You are not your organization. You may have overlap, but there is an individual in there who needs to be fulfilled.

7. **If you are miserable at work, it may not be your employer's fault.**

For sure, it could be their fault. They could be underpaying you or not developing you or making you come into the office on Saturdays. But if your employer is doing what they can and you're still unhappy, you might lack purpose. Consider why you work, and what you want to get out of work. If you don't know the answers to those questions, you should. Once you do, consider whether it's possible to achieve that in your current working relationship. If not, it's time to move on.

8. **If your employees are chronically unhappy, you may not be validating their purpose.**

You should. (If you haven't already, see the chapter on reciprocity.)

9. **If you don't know what your employees' individual purposes are, you should.**

Ask them during annual reviews or one-on-ones. Ask them to be honest, and trust them to share. If you want to open the door, share your own without the corporate bullshit. (For more on this, check out "Ask It Yourself.")

A purposeful diagnostic

Purpose is a personal journey. While employers cannot cultivate purpose for an employee, they can integrate purpose discovery and strategy into their interactions and evaluations. Learning more about an employee's purpose, and having employees who have a more defined sense of purpose, can help you formulate investment and development strategies that will better resonate with their goals and interests (reciprocity), and better address their professional uncertainties (continuity).

For employees, here are three questions you can ask of yourself. For leaders, you can encourage your employees to consider these same questions. I've included some probing questions after each question to jump-start things if the initial question seems vague. I've also included my answers to these questions, taken from my actual professional development conversations with mentors.

1. ***What are your non-negotiables?*** (Probe: What are the things you absolutely need from a job? What are the things that, if a job didn't have them, you would definitely walk away?)

   Example: I have three. First, fortune and glory. I want to be able to prosper so that I can do more than just provide for my family and myself (e.g., go to Disney World), and I want to do so in a way and in a place that will help me build my skills, expertise, and reputation. Second, autonomy. I don't want to be micromanaged. I want to be worthy with and for people who trust me when I've given them reason to do so. Third, flexibility. If your reasoning is "this is the way we've always done things," we probably won't be a good match. I want to be able to experiment with ideas and try new things.

2. ***What makes you get out of bed in the morning?*** (Probe: What are your "so-that's"? Even if your job isn't perfect, and even if you'd rather be doing something else, what motivates you to try?)

   Example: I like solving puzzles. I like doing research because it's practical puzzle-solving. I absolutely hate being bored, so I'm always looking for stimulation in the form of a problem to be solved. I also like being reliable and being relied upon. I want to be the person people go to with questions. If I don't get out of bed, how can I be available? And to be totally candid, I'm not independently wealthy and I have bills to pay and things I want to do that cost money.

3. ***What is your best next step?*** (Probe: What is one reasonable thing you can do to move your purpose forward? Can you start today? If not, what's stopping you?)

Example: Finish this book.

HOPE

Hope is the optimism that things can change, and the will to pursue that change, despite the odds.

Hope and lonely funerals

I spent a summer working at a Buddhist temple in northern Japan. My job was a product of the graying community: I was to attend funerals and memorial services of people who had few living relatives, friends, neighbors, or acquaintances to see them across the river. I would sit for the service, light a stick of incense, and say a small prayer. If the deceased's grave was on the premises, I would visit it, leaving another stick and another prayer. On one occasion, the only attendees were myself and the deceased's work friend, long retired. I sat on the family's side of the temple for the funeral, to even out the spacing and, according to the priest's wife, to make the spirit think family had visited. On another occasion, the only mourners were the priest's daughter and myself.

Earlier in the summer, over a great deal of beer, the head priest had told me that he was uncertain if people actually had souls or spirits, and if anything actually happened when people died. He couldn't be sure, he said ruefully, because he hadn't died yet as far as he could remember. In his perspective, the point of doing funerals wasn't for the deceased—*"nakunatta hito ha nakunatta da yo,"* the dead were dead. Funerals, memorial services, gravestones, and all of the other trappings of post-mortem rituals were for those left behind. The point of a funeral was to bring people together as a tangible reminder that a community still existed. Yes, the community had a new hole now, one that could never fully be mended, but the fabric of that community was still there, still in need of tending, and still worth the effort.

After one of the lonely funerals, I asked the head priest what was the point of having a funeral if there wasn't any community left. One person didn't make a community. The priest's daughter and I were just proxies for the deceased's loved ones. What were we really accomplishing by holding a funeral among ourselves? "Because," the priest said, "it's better than doing nothing."

I thought about the priest's explanation often that summer. In many ways, the village the temple served seemed like a hopeless case. Like many rural areas in Japan, the village was depopulating as young people moved to bigger cities for college and employment, rarely if ever to return, and older residents died off. While some villages in other parts of the country had tried to effect a "hometown revival," none had really panned out. In any case, the village in question didn't have the resources to try. There was no industry to speak of, extant or incoming. Even the farms had largely stopped producing. It was a dying community waiting for the end.

But it also wasn't. Despite the inevitable, some residents still tried. The temple continued to tend to the community, hosting events in the great hall (a showing of *Jaws* was a highlight that summer). A group of elderly citizens formed a committee that went door to door checking on residents, spreading cheer, and inviting folks to weekly get-togethers at the community center. There was a local men's baseball team, and although they rarely had enough people to fill a bench (or opponents to consistently play), they practiced regularly. For those who remained, it was all better than doing nothing.

Doing something was how a dying community in a bleak part of Japan kindled hope. While the activities they planned and initiatives they launched were unlikely to save their village, they were able to change circumstances for those who remained, even if just to create a little extra warmth. Hope was both their belief in the possibility of change, and the intentional actions they took every day to make that change a reality, despite the odds.

Hope, practically speaking

In a world driven by hard data, measurable indicators, and tangible results, hope can seem abstract. Impractical. But, hope is *practical*. Incredibly so. Without hope, work just wouldn't happen.

When you really think about it, most work is absurd. For every farmer or firefighter who contributes directly to our survival, there are many more workers who are building widgets, trading widgets, or writing stories about the widgets (like me!). What's the point of all this industry? In the grand scheme of things, does all this effort matter? Maybe. We *hope* so. Otherwise we just wouldn't do it. We may not know for certain the significance of our work, but those who work are, as a rule, not nihilistic. Even if we can't articulate it, we have some underlying belief that our work, as an extension of our lives, means something. Work is absurd, but it is hopeful.

Hope is the belief that things can change *for the better*. Hope is a feeling, a baseline optimism that things will work out.

Hope is not groundless; we draw on evidence to underwrite the soundness of our beliefs. We *hope* our job at a 100-year-old company is stable *because* if the business has lasted this long, it probably isn't going anywhere. We *hope* majoring in AI technologies will be rewarding *because* everyone is talking about its importance for the future. We *hope* we will get a raise this year *because* we got one last year, and it was a strong quarter.

Of course, there are no guarantees that any of these hopes will pan out. That's what gives them hope. But our belief in the potential of positive outcomes is so powerful that we will endeavor without a signed contract.

Hope is essential for working relationships because it empowers us to manage the risk that is inherent in these connections. Risk and hope animate continuity, reciprocity, and purpose. We accept a job offer, *risking* that it could be a toxic environment or we could get laid off after four months, because we *hope* it's a good job. We *risk* specializing in an industry because we *hope* it will make us valuable.

We give to someone, *risking* that they won't reciprocate, because we *hope* they will. We *risk* trying because we *hope* we will succeed. Without hope, risk would grind us to a halt.

Movement is critical. Hope is both the belief that things can change for the better, and **the will to pursue that change**. Hope is active.

Students of Japanese culture (and dinner guests) are often surprised to hear that the highest rates of suicide in Japan are not school-aged children (despite being the most sensationalized in domestic and international media), but rather retirement-aged men. Having identities and lives deeply tied to their work persona, when these men find themselves without a job—be it planned retirement or forced—many become lost. They have nothing to do, and thus no purpose, nothing to offer their friends or family, nothing keeping them stable. They have no reason for being. So they end it.

Working in a community that had four times the national suicide rate, the aforementioned head priest's words have a greater weight: It's better to do something than nothing. Indeed, one of the strategies of government healthcare centers in rural Japan to lower suicide rates is to engage retirement-aged men in meaningful activities, work around the community that needs doing, and needs them to do it.

We practice hope. We encourage ourselves and others to persist through tough situations by sharing hopeful mantras: It can't be like this forever. The market has to turn around eventually. It's only a matter of time! Things will get better. You'll land on your feet. We also leverage hope to push ourselves forward and take the next right step. If you've ever gotten yourself out of bed at the end of a particularly shitty week, you've successfully practiced hope.

The pandemic was a practical lesson in practical hope: trying new strategies to stay afloat, betting that you can make it until the furlough ends, waiting on a vaccine that will get things back to normal. Some of the outcomes we hoped for came true, and some didn't. Even so, we persisted, despite the crises and the panic and having no living precedent to cite in support of our beliefs.

Hope often runs automatically in the background of our everyday lives, essential but unnoticed, like breathing. But, like breathing, we can concentrate on it, changing it to an intentional action. Becoming more mindful of our practice of hope and its impact on our lives and the lives of those around us is essential for cultivating resilient working relationships.

Practicing hope

Hope is a lot like yogic breathing. For sure, you can go all day breathing without really thinking about it. It's convenient that such an important life-sustaining function can run in the background. But there are a lot of benefits to becoming more mindful about your breathing: Purposeful breathing can ground us, calm us, make us more mindful of the world around us and what's going on inside us.

Hope is similar. It's an automatic process that informs our decisions and mindset. Most of us get out of bed and go to work without going through a set of hopeful affirmations. Our belief that things can change for the better is tacit, and our will to push toward that change is reflexive. But, you can also be very intentional about practicing hope. You can, for example, sit on the edge of your bed in the morning and recite the things you have to look forward to, the big changes on the horizon, how you're going to make a difference today, etc. Gratitude journaling has become increasingly popular in the world of work (promoted by LinkedIn and TikTok influencers alike), the practice of writing down and reflecting on things you feel thankful for. Bullet journaling has a similar ethos: a confidence-building statement on what you will (or hope to) accomplish today. Social media is full of people sharing hopeful anecdotes—"I got 99 rejections, but then I got the perfect offer" stories on LinkedIn, for example—to both remind themselves and inspire others (and get those delicious clicks).

This isn't even a new trend: "Hang in there" cat posters, the cliche decor of HR departments and guidance counselor offices across the country, are a classic affirmation that better days are coming. The intention isn't for the cat to hang there indefinitely.

Like yogic breathing, an intentional approach to hope has many benefits. As someone who struggles with clinical depression, I've made a practice of assuring myself that things can get better by taking an inventory of all the things that have turned out okay, of the things I have accomplished, of the times others have come through, despite my worries. It helps. For me, hope is an evidence-based science. And reflecting on the experience that gives me hope has the knock-on effect of inspiring gratitude for others and for myself. It reminds me of my connection to other people at times when I feel loss and alienation. If you've ever experienced hopelessness, you know what being swallowed by a black tide feels like. If you've had the fortune to come up for air, you also know the power of rekindling hope.

I can't tell you how to practice hope. Like all aspects of our working relationships, hope is a deeply personal thing. I *can* tell you that journaling or blog posting or cat posters aren't really my thing. I can also share the common threads I've observed in the successful practices of others, elements that I've incorporated into my own practice that, so far, have worked well for me.

In my research, highly effective practices of hope are three things: (1) active, in that you actively engage in the thing, (2) immersive, in that it takes you out of the day-to-day and transports you to a more hopeful place, and (3) practical. This last one may be more personal preference, but I would argue from research and personal experience that the most sustainable practices reward the practitioner with some practical takeaway—a new skill, a new experience, a new connection.

Learning is by far the most effective and accessible practice of hope. Good learning checks all the boxes: It's active, it's immersive, and you take away something practical. Learning itself is also a deeply hopeful endeavor. The impetus of learning presumes that learners can change, and that the things they learn can change the world. Old dogs can't learn new tricks? That's bullshit. Everyone can learn at any time. There's no age limit or title requirement to actively engage in learning. It just takes time, effort, and a learning goal worth pursuing.

The recognition that I was learning sustained me and grounded me in my career journey as an anthropologist of work, a winding road that took me through researching work to working while researching to doing research on work professionally (a journey of ultimately learning how to do research *on* work *at* work *for* work). Learning activates hope by demonstrating our capacity to change for the better. Even when the learning curve is steep and the road is hard, looking back at the distance we've traveled proves that we can make progress. Looking back through my field notes over the past decade, the transformation is striking.

This doesn't mean that practicing hope—through learning or otherwise—is easy. It's not. It's often an ass kicking. Nor is our change always so noticeable. Change can be subtle, sometimes frustratingly so. Nor is practicing hope linear. There are a lot of steps forward, and also a lot of steps back. It can feel like you're going in circles. There were days in the brewery or in the field where I felt like I was standing still. But learning always has a forward momentum, even if it's too slow to identify in real time, like the rotation of the Earth.

Change is a wheel that never stops turning. Practicing hope is about trying to feel the turning beneath our feet, and moving with that change toward a better future. Every step makes us a little stronger, a little wiser, a little different. Every rotation brings us a little closer to paradise.

Creating hopeful spaces

Hope can also be a collective practice. Hope takes on a different dimension when you work to inspire hope in others. Leaders can strive to create hopeful spaces for themselves and their employees. If you are a leader, consider this: Is your working environment conducive to hope? Does your organization create a space where you, your employees, and your customers feel it is okay to be hopeful? If not, don't lose hope; that just means there's work to be done.

A space that welcomes and encourages hope is one that embraces change. Hopeful spaces welcome new ideas, techniques, and strategies. They support personal and collective growth. They are willing to take different perspectives. Most important, they are not afraid of failure, and they do not punish people for taking a reasonable risk that doesn't pan out.

In my experience, academia is not a particularly hopeful space. Even though the point of college and graduate school is ostensibly to experiment, take risks, grow, and fail—the learning process—that wasn't always the case. Conventional thinking was often celebrated. Research and writing should follow approved patterns. Long lists of citations were a prerequisite to knowing what you were talking about. It wasn't like this all the time, but change was stifled enough that it was hard to miss a distinct strain of conformity in academic culture.

Unlike many of my classmates, and later colleagues, I was fortunate in that I had direct advisors who, despite the pressure of sameness, took pains to inspire hope when I needed it the most.

Case Study: A tale of two failures

"I WANT YOU TO GET OUT!" the vice priest screamed, billowing his black robe for emphasis like a furious bat.

It was the summer, 2012. I was three months encamped in a Buddhist temple in rural northern Japan, studying the organizational dynamics of these community institutions. I was evaluating the readiness of temples to serve as emergency relief shelters in the aftermath of large-scale disasters for remote and underserved farming villages. In the wake of the 2011 Tōhoku earthquake, tsunami, and nuclear meltdown, it was a timely project. To map out the organization, I worked at the temple (fetching tea, gardening, and attending funerals as a proxy mourner), interviewing the head priest and vice priest, their families, long-suffering volunteers, parishioners, next-door neighbors, the gardener, mourners visiting from out of town, members of the community baseball team who practiced in the temple's parking lot, and just about anyone who would tolerate a conversation with my halting Japanese. It was this canvassing that sparked the vice priest's ire. In his opinion, if I was interested in understanding how the temple worked, it should be sufficient—and I should be thankful, he added—to talk to the person at—or at least near—the top. Why was I talking to these lackeys and tourists? Wasn't *his* expertise good enough? I was actively disrespecting his authority. I was making him look like a fool.

I tried to explain the nature of my research (I had prior to starting the project, but I thought I'd try again), but the vice-priest wouldn't budge. He gave me an ultimatum: Restrict my research to interviews with him or get out. The head priest and his wife, sitting around the shared table, said nothing. The vice priest wasn't just their employee, he was their son-in-law. They didn't want to rock the boat any more than it already was. I tried appealing to his reason one last time, but the vice priest refused. By way of driving home his point, he reminded me that it wasn't just my project—it was also my career—that was contingent on his support. My frustration got the better of me and I told him what I thought of his expertise. The vice priest shouted for me to get out, so I left.

I passed into my room at a nearby inn in a daze. Numbly, I typed out an email to my advisor, John. I told him what happened and how I responded, how I had lost my research site. I worried about what this would do to my academic and professional prospects. I apologized for messing it all up. I was so embarrassed. I sent the message, then lay on the ground and waited for John to receive it in Texas. I was sure I was finished.

John's reply came eight agonizing hours later. It wasn't what I expected. I'll paraphrase from memory:

"Aaron, sorry to hear about that, but it sounds like an interesting experience! The vice priest sounds like an ass. Now it's time to think like an anthropologist. Why do you think he reacted that way? What might be going on behind the scenes? Your real project starts here. Good luck and happy researching!

No anger. No condemnation. He didn't want me to pack it up

and head home. Rather, he was sympathetic, if not mildly amused and overtly curious. He expressed some sympathy and then got to business. He reminded me of why I was there, who I was, and what I could do. It was pitch-perfect, exactly what I needed to hear.

I picked myself up, went to the local coffee shop, and started writing out my notes. Word got around the village that I had been ejected from the temple. Seeing an opportunity, parishioners, neighbors, and family friends visited me at the cafe, invited me to bars, and took me on long drives. They wanted to tell their side of the story. Trouble was—and had been—brewing in the temple for some time. So close to the temple, I wasn't someone they could trust with their worries. But nothing had changed—I was outside. The anxieties they vented, the dynamics they revealed, and the hopes they expressed became the foundation of my first thesis, and for my research career.

Years later. Another university, another project, another advisor, another disaster. My daughter had come early, too early for her lungs to develop fully. She spent nearly three months in the NICU. Lauren and I visited the hospital down the street every day. Lauren took a leave of absence from work, and I buried myself in brewing when I wasn't with Elsie or sleeping in our shitty apartment. She was discharged two days before Christmas, on oxygen. We spent the next three months monitoring her progress, battling with acid reflux, and generally trying our best to finally enjoy being parents while also trying to avoid a return to the NICU.

My research was finished. I was supposed to be writing. Consumed by this crisis, I just didn't. I didn't write a word for nearly eight months.

When Elsie was finally out of the woods, I worked up the courage to sit down with my advisor and talk about next steps, how I would recover, and what kind of future in academia I could expect. I anticipated a stern lecture about the consequences of my unexpected furlough. At the very least, I expected him to openly worry as to my career prospects. After all, I had been on track throughout my coursework and research, consistently making progress. Now I had stalled, my momentum lost. I was sure I was fucked.

I said as much to my advisor. Chris passed my anxiety with a shrug. "You're still on track," he said calmly, rotating a coffee cup. "You'll be fine."

He went on to talk about the positives. For one, even though it was a rough road, Elsie was home now. Two, I had been working at the brewery the whole time, and could add those experiences to my project. Third, the whole episode had probably given me a very different perspective, a deeper, more interesting view on the subject of my research.

Chris's words cut through months of anxiety over my daughter, my dissertation, and my future. If someone I respected so much had this much confidence in me, then maybe I really would be fine. Chris was right; I finished my dissertation and graduated on track. While academia didn't ultimately pan out, my priorities had shifted to professional research anyway. The months of turtling up with Elsie also served an unexpected purpose; not only were we pros at quarantine by the time COVID-19 came around, we were also able to face the pandemic—and the job insecurity and economic instability that followed in its wake—with a healthy degree of optimism. After all, we had been through something even more challenging before, and we had adapted and come through it stronger. We were hopeful.

Modeling hope

Two different advisors, two different crises, and two different conversations, but with the same through line of empathy and encouragement. I think about these conversations often. They might have been passing moments for John and Chris, unremarkable, but they've indelibly colored my interactions with students in the university, mentees in the industry, and my daughter at home. They taught me how to roll with failure. How to reframe disappointment and dysfunction into opportunity. How to see hope from a sea of change.

As individuals, we need to accept that the cost of pursuing change is sometimes failure. Hope is the willingness to absorb that cost. We also need to form working relationships with those individuals and organizations that inspire our hope. It's a struggle to maintain belief that things will change for the better in a place that never seems to change. Worse, in a place that balks at or actively shoots down any change they notice. Sure, it's possible change could happen in these seemingly hopeless places, but it's not sustainable. It shouldn't be acceptable.

If you are a leader, then you have the capacity to create hopeful spaces. One of the aforementioned advisors, Chris, encouraged his graduate students to read not just academic books, but to always have an interesting book in progress. His rationale: "Reading makes you a better person." My interpretation: People who read new things are willing to encounter new ideas. As a leader, you can model hope by embracing change. I worked with a faculty member who would go around the table after he asked a question, sourcing everyone's perspective and offering a reflection on each in return. He wasn't afraid to encounter a differing opinion or a radical point of view. That was the whole point of bringing people together to work on a shared project. Open up the floor and see what happens.

You can also model hope by embracing failure. Brewers were often great at this. Between the creative ethos of craft production and the egalitarian camaraderie of artisans, brewers would often reminisce in impromptu retrospectives on all the beers they brewed that missed the mark, or all the times they demonstrated "what not to do" by making a critical error. I once went to a tasting party with a group of local brewers and other brewery staff. The head brewer of the hosting brewery passed around pints of his new experimental beer. It tasted awful—way too piney and way too sweet. "It's pretty bad, right?" the brewer said.

Early in my research, I reached between a manifold of pipes in front of the brew kettle to close a valve. The manifold was boiling hot wort; in a moment of carelessness, I caught my bare skin on the exposed metal, searing a small lopsided circle into the underside of my arm. I swore. The head brewer noticed my reaction, then the wound, and laughed. "That's your first real injury," he said, his voice tinged with what almost sounded like pride. "Now you're one of us." He and the other brewer then proceeded to show off the numerous faded cuts, burns, and scrapes that traced their own arms and legs. Fucking up was how you learned to be a real brewer.

Holding regular retrospectives on completed projects is a similarly effective strategy in office culture. My current employer uses three simple categories: what went well, what could be improved, and big takeaways. The reality is that rarely—if ever—is a project totally successful or totally a failure. Some things worked, and some things didn't. Some things worked really well, and some things were a disaster. Consider all of it. Identify and retain the good ideas, don't repeat the bad ones. It's a process of trial and error. Errors are necessary to the equation.

It's practices and attitudes like these that inspire hope in others. By embracing risk and reframing failure as a learning moment, you empower others to change, modeling the confidence that their attempts to grow, even if met with temporary setbacks, won't end in disaster.

Averting the Great Stagnation

We live in an age of the "Great This" and "Great That," cultural movements and social moments sensationalized into defining characteristics of the world of work. They can be annoying and tend to oversimplify the dynamics at play. But they are also super-catchy and sticky in readers' memories. So I made one too! It's called the Great Stagnation, and it describes the gradual atrophy of work.

There's nothing new under the sun. It's a familiar truism that isn't really true. We encounter new ideas and things all the time. Sure, they may have similarities to past things—an airplane and a dirigible are both flying machines—but they're not the same. Change, even when incremental, creates something novel. Innovation does innovate.

But imagine a world in which nobody innovated. Instead, everyone just latched on to the most statistically or anecdotally sound best practices and contented themselves with implementing those practices again and again. In his book, *A Humble Guide to Fixing Everything in Brand, Marketing, and Sales*, Bret Starr writes that the road to hell is paved with optimization. That hell is not just for bad branding. It's a workers' hell. One in which the potential of true change is eschewed for slightly tweaked repetition. The only risks are technical glitches or miscommunications. The only growth is efficiency and profit.

If this sounds like a nightmare scenario to you, me too. But this is a nightmare that can be avoided. We don't have to work that way. In fact, thankfully, few of us do. But in a world of blocking and tackling and incremental SaaS products, big ideas can seem like overly risky endeavors, especially on a balance sheet. There are many incentives to follow the herd; "nobody ever got fired for buying IBM" is as much an endorsement of groupthink as it is a commendation of IBM's products. In the years since the pandemic, this ethos has only grown more enticing. Keep your head down, turtle up, don't make big moves, and wait for the pendulum to swing back to bullish times. If a critical mass of big players and powerful CEOs are doing it, it can't be wrong. And even if it is, you'll be wrong together. There's safety in the herd. The only problem is you're surrounded by a bunch of cows.

I imagine the logical conclusion of the herd optimization ethos: a world devoid of innovation, monotonous and routinized, a hundred shades of beige. At what point does work become so risk averse, change sensitive, so boring that workers disengage entirely?

American companies are already struggling with engagement. Leaders wonder why their employees don't show initiative or passion, growing frustrated with teams of box-checkers and order-takers. Discretionary effort is down. So is retention. Burnout is rampant. Japanese work culture has been facing a similar dilemma since the early 2000s. Bright young professionals bust ass through school and college to get their dream job in a big company, only to find that the work is boring and unfulfilling. Japan's artisan movement is fueled by former white-collar employees who got sick of it and quit. When describing their previous work environment, they used a common phrase: "*muimi*." Meaningless.

What's the point of doing pointless work? Why give discretionary effort when that added energy goes nowhere? Why bring your full self to work if you can get by with your half self, or quarter self?

A routine complaint among brewers at larger, more established craft breweries was that there was no room for creativity. The brewery had its flagship and seasonal lineups set, the recipes dialed in, and the process fine-tuned. Come in, brew to script, go home, repeat. Turnover for assistant and mid-level brewers who realized they were working on a glorified assembly line was high. I worked with a brewery that, after a particularly churn-heavy summer, decided to address the lack of creative agency by installing a pilot system. Any employee with sufficient training could use the small-scale brewing system on off-hours to create their own recipes. They could use surplus ingredients as they liked, and supplement with their own ingredients. If a majority of the staff gave the finished beer a thumbs-up, it would go on one of two taps in the taproom reserved for the pilot brew program. It was a huge success. The pilot system was constantly busy, retention and productivity surged, and the brewery became a sought-after job in the area, especially for entry-level professionals.

If you're a business leader struggling with engagement, consider this: Does your organization inspire hope? Do you cultivate an environment in which meaningful change is embraced? In which failure that arises from good-faith effort is reframed as learning? If your answer is "no," or if you're not sure, this is where to start. Roundtable a concept. Host a retro. Take a page from the brewery's book and do something to generate discussion, spark imagination, and get change flowing.

People work because they are hopeful. People are hopeful because there is the possibility of change. If you remove the possibility of change, hope crumbles and the impetus to work dies. If you want to solve your engagement problem and help avert the Great Stagnation, cultivate hope.

A RELATIONAL FRAMEWORK

ALL TOGETHER NOW

"It is interesting to contemplate a tangled bank, clothed with many plants of many kinds, with birds singing on the bushes, with various insects flitting about, and with worms crawling through the damp earth, and to reflect that these elaborately constructed forms, so different from each other, and dependent upon each other in so complex a manner, have all been produced by laws acting around us."
- Charles Darwin

Workplace Voltron

The elements of working relationships are like Voltron. Continuity, reciprocity, purpose, and hope can be distinct parts of a functioning whole insofar as they each have individual identities and functions. In practice, however, like the climax of nearly every *kaiju* battle, these elements combine in a mutually influencing super-robot-style synthesis that ultimately develops, sustains, or undermines the resilience of working relationships and their capacity to absorb change.

Continuity, reciprocity, purpose, and hope are components of the same engine that drives working relationships and ultimately drives workplace success: When all of the parts are expertly maintained, the engine runs well. But when even one element is neglected, it can begin to not only malfunction, but damage other parts in the process.

The interplay of these elements makes our relationship to work complex. While the previous four chapters look at each element in turn, this chapter considers how continuity, reciprocity, purpose, and hope mesh and function together, for better and for worse.

Knock-on effects

The engine analogy also has its limitations. Wheres the parts of a machine are physically distinct and can be individually cataloged, the elements of working relationships overlap and blur together. It is often difficult to tell where reciprocity begins and hope ends, or whether professional development conversations serve continuity or purpose. (In actuality, professional development activates all four elements.) You may have already suspected this from the common thread of investment that links generating reciprocity and creating hopeful spaces.

In truth, it would be harder—if not impossible—to influence one element without ultimately impacting another. This interdependence has three consequences (or virtues, depending on how you look at it):

1. It complicates the situation. It's not really possible to talk practically about one element without implicating the others. If you were looking for a tidy strategy, this won't be a good use case for you. Working relationships in the field are not conducive to sharp demarcation.

2. It simplifies matters. Paradoxically, perhaps, the interdependence of continuity et al. means that pulling on one thread will pull on all of the others. You don't need to create four different strategies to improve four different metrics.

3. It creates an environment prone to knock-on effects.

Knock-on effects are cumulative impacts that result from an initial action, an added, often indirect result that adds weight to the things we do. In working relationships, continuity, reciprocity, purpose, and hope constantly spark subsequent reactions in other areas of the relationship. What this means is that attempts to influence one element of working relationships can easily snowball into shaping other aspects of the working relationship, for better or worse. What this also means is that if your approach to interpersonal relationships in the workplace is akin to a bull in a china shop, bad news. As mutually influenced elements, if you screw up continuity or reciprocity, it's going to have an impact on purpose and hope.

Take continuity, for example. Continuity is the trust that working relationships will endure. A stable organization—one that doesn't look like it's going to close or lay people off anytime soon—fosters a sense of reliability. Working relationships forged with such a company will likely be more durable. A relationship that is likely to stand the test of time is worth investing in, as it is more likely that the investment will eventually and/or repeatedly pay dividends. If an employee feels a business is sustainable, profitable, and growing, they will be more willing to give discretionary effort because, like a borrower with great credit who consistently keeps their promises, the business is good for it. A high-functioning organization will also be more likely to have the resources to properly reciprocate by compensating, recognizing, rewarding, and developing employees.

This same relationship can backfire if a seemingly successful and stable organization is stingy with pay, bonuses, or development opportunities. If leadership consistently announces that they're crushing it, that everything is on the up, that they're getting record profits, etc., but doesn't *show* that with proper reciprocation, that company's leaders are either greedy—and thus not worthy of forming a reciprocal relationship with—or liars who aren't doing nearly as well as they claim, and thus not likely to provide continuity.

Continuity also serves as the foundation for purpose and hope. A stable relationship to work is necessary to develop a sense of purpose and make progress toward achieving it. Likewise, that relationship would also have to stick around long enough to be meaningfully changeable, and for that change to trend toward the better. An organization constantly lurching from one crisis to the next would not be a solid ground to pursue purpose or hope, nor would someone devoid of marketable skills be able to get a foothold gainful enough to develop either.

Consider hope. Actively developing profitable skills, contributions being recognized, and making noticeable progress toward—or even fulfilling—a purpose; those are all powerful evidence to suggest that things *can* change, and change for the better. If things can change for the better, then there is the grounds for hope. Hope is also a motivator. The will to reach toward positive change (a will spurred by past precedent) inspires people to keep trying, to push harder, to take chances, and to see opportunity where others see only problems.

Hopelessness will crush a working relationship. What's the point of investing in a relationship that doesn't pay off by growing? What's the point of getting out of bed if nothing you do makes progress toward your goals? What's the point of working for an organization, no matter how established, that has completely stagnated? You can see the answers to these questions in plummeting retention rates and chronic disengagement, or the listlessness and ennui of so many millennial and Gen Z workers.

Reciprocity indexes a relationship that is worth *continuing to* invest in; the cycle of giving, receiving, and reciprocating is a living justification that there is substance to the interaction and the potential for growth. To give and not receive would be like throwing money into a bottomless hole: pointless, hopeless, and ultimately unsustainable.

With purpose, working relationships have a reason to be. Without purpose, while it may be nice that an organization is established, that your work bears fruit, or that things are changing, none of it matters in the long run.

Here's a handy diagram of the constructive and destructive knock-on effects the presence or absence of an element can have on the *whole*:

Constructive cycles	Destructive cycles
Continuity makes relationships feasible	Discontinuity undermines confidence in the relationship
Reciprocity makes relationships perpetual	One-sidedness makes relationships transactional
Purpose makes relationships meaningful	A lack of purpose makes relationships pointless
Hope makes relationships logical	Hopelessness makes relationships illogical

Knock-on effects also factor in at the whole relationship level, in which one working relationship can have an upstream or downstream effect on other relationships. We see this in role models whose commitment to their craft or people inspire us to take similar approaches to work. We also see this in grassroots movements, where popular consensus around how something ought to be done or how people ought to be treated bubble up to inform organizational policy.

This is also why offering certain high-impact benefits like career transition services can have a halo effect, improving the perceptions of employees who never have and never will use the benefit. Because all relationships are interconnected in the tangled banks of our working lives, what happens to one has implications for all. This is true when these relationships succeed, and even more pronounced when relationships fail.

When the chain snaps

When working relationships fail, the results are often spectacular. Our relationships to work are like lengths of chain or cars: When they do their job well, they become utterly unremarkable. However, when the chain snaps or the car breaks down, we suddenly realize how critical it was because of the profound impact its absence has on our life. Working relationships generally go without saying because they come without saying; they are so fundamental to the weft and weave of our working lives that they become almost automatic, and typically become most noticeable—and studyable—when they fall apart.

Moments of relationship collapse reveal a great deal about the interconnectedness of continuity, reciprocity, purpose, and hope. While we may not use those exact terms, principals and observers often cite the elements of working relationships as the root cause of the disaster.

Take, for example, the seemingly out-of-touch CEO who became momentarily infamous in the spring of 2023 when she responded to employee worries about bonuses by telling them to "leave pity city." [22] The internet exploded with obvious complaints about the CEO being ungrateful to her staff (reciprocity) and speculations that the CEO would lose her job or the company would suffer because of her bad take (continuity). A colleague brought up an interesting additional layer: "I wouldn't want to work for her," they said. "If after everything we went through with the pandemic, that's still your attitude? Wow." In other words, if the shit show that was the pandemic and its immediate aftermath didn't soften her approach to employee uncertainty, what would? Some people never change, and a place without change is hopeless.

Similar speculation occurred in the wake of high-profile layoffs in which organizations and leaders seemed to be competing for the most inhuman approach to severing a relationship. Following the seemingly hopeful sign of a $750 million cash infusion, the Better.com CEO laid off 15% of his staff in a one-way Zoom conference. [23] Employees were

---

[22] In case you missed it, see Emily Olson's piece in NPR, "'Leave pity city,' Miller-Knoll CEO tells staff who asked whether they'd lose bonuses" (2023).

[23] See Jack Kelly's descriptively titled "CEO Who Fired 900 Employees Via A Zoom Video And Called His Employees 'Dumb Dolphins' Had A Mass Layoff—Some Workers Found Out By Seeing Their Bank Account," Forbes (2022).

heartbroken, the wider world of work was outraged, and several senior executives resigned. The CEO took a leave of absence—or a vacation, depending on who you ask—to reflect and get in touch with his values.

Some Google employees didn't even get the courtesy of a strained video fireside chat. They received emails notifying them that they were let go. Those who didn't check their inboxes found out through other means, like being denied entry to the office when their ID cards repeatedly flashed red at the door.[24] Twitter staff came to a similar realization when they were locked out of company computers and email.[25]

Less high-profile severances are no less traumatic for the person experiencing it. I worked with a career transition firm that shared customer testimonials as part of the research project. The pain, humiliation, and worry of their professional clients—people operating at levels at which you could be forgiven for assuming they would have a golden parachute—was palpable. Having been laid off from previous positions, and having friends and colleagues be laid off, the anxiety and embarrassment hit close to home.

On the other side of the equation, these case studies make me wonder what's going wrong in the working relationships of these CEOs and organizations that empowers them to behave in ways that are so brazenly shitty. There probably isn't a "good" way to lay someone off, but there are certainly very awful and callous ways of doing it. And recent examples have presented a master class in what not to do if you want to look like you have even the semblance of a conscience or soul. But the question stands: Are their futures so shaky, their relationships so precarious, are they so desperate that even seemingly heartless moves have an internal logic to them? Are their working relationships so tenuous that they have nothing left to lose? Are they so burned out

---

[24] Aaron Mok, Kate Duffy, and Sawdah Bhaimiya, "Some Google employees didn't realize they were laid off until their badges wouldn't let them into the office," Business Insider (2023).

[25] Grace Kay, "Some Twitter staff reportedly found out they were laid off after they couldn't log in to their laptops or email," Business Insider (2023).

on their work that they just don't care anymore? Are they so secure in their positions of power and influence that they've become out of touch with the relationships that enabled their rise and sustained their authority?

I don't know. I haven't interviewed any of them, and the interviews that I have seen all read like corporate PR ass-covering. A degree of inaccessibility comes with being in those positions of power. However, no matter how high you climb, you're never beyond the influence of working relationships—your own relationship to work, and your relationships to the people and organizations and industries you work with.

This is also a good opportunity to return to knock-on effects. Just as problems with working relationships among employees can cause drops in engagement or retention that flow up to cause major organizational problems, so too can fissures in the working relationships of leadership—especially highly influential executives—flow down and destabilize the working relationships of many. When it comes to working relationships, we all need to have our shit together.

Delicate, but durable

Having read up to this point, you might be worrying that your working relationships are hanging by a thread, that any number of things expected or unexpected could swoop in and overturn the apple cart in an instant. When we look at the collapse of working relationships in retrospect, it can definitely seem like that. However, in the actual flow of work, where working relationships are developed and shaped little by little, step by step, success and failure are exceedingly more incremental. Rome wasn't built in a day, nor was it destroyed in a night, despite what the poets say.

Despite their weaknesses, working relationships are quite durable. Momentary and even sustained lapses in any one of the four elements can be weathered. Indeed, lapses often come with the costs of doing business. But these lapses can also be opportunities to highlight and improve other elements of the relationship.

For example, if a company has a layoff, a downturn in continuity is inevitable. Nor is that downturn likely to be quickly resolved. An organization can't fix continuity at the time of a layoff; confidence in the stability of a relationship has to be gradually rebuilt over time. Even so, remaining employees can continue to experience reciprocity, purpose, and hope through a layoff. A business stumbling can be an opportunity to show up for those left behind, to refocus around a common mission, and to position and prepare the people who will be the future of the company. For those let go, formal and informal career transition efforts can extend reciprocity, purpose, and hope, maintaining the relationship despite the crisis. In one study I conducted on behalf of a client, we found that employees who received career transition services from their former employers were significantly more likely to see their former employers as empathetic, and significantly more likely to return as boomerang employees.

If you're a business leader and you're looking at what to do after a layoff, you might think you need to take immediate action toward fixing your employees' confidence in your organization. You do need to fix your continuity, but in time. Focus instead on what you can impact now: reciprocity, purpose, and hope. I've observed multiple times that the most effective way to bolster continuity in the aftermath of a crisis that fundamentally disrupts that continuity is to bolster all of the elements that surround continuity. If people still have reciprocity, hope, and purpose, and maybe even a renewed sense of those, their relationships will carry through the lull in continuity.

A layoff is just one example. What about a promotion that isn't what you imagined? I worked with an apprentice brewer who dreamed of working at a large craft brewery with the latest technology, shiny taprooms, and money to spend on marketing. He got what he wanted, but it wasn't what he expected. The creative scrappiness of his former role was replaced by something more akin to a factory production job. However, the pay was a significant step up from his previous position, as were the professional development opportunities. For the first time in his life, he was making enough money to pay his bills and had a trajectory.

Just as employers can draw on different elements of working relationships to compensate for weaknesses, employees can do the same to positively shape their own relationships. In his work on medical care professionals volunteering for Médecins Sans Frontières (MSF, also known as Doctors Without Borders), Peter Redfield finds that while MSF provides little in the way of the reciprocity that for-profit organizations can provide and often places volunteers in unstable geopolitical spaces, doctors are nevertheless inspired to give discretionary effort across multiple tours, driven by the purpose to heal and the belief that they can make a difference.[26] While working relationships between volunteers and MSF can be sustained by purpose and hope alone, Redfield finds that volunteers gradually become disillusioned with their mission when they see their efforts eclipsed by the sheer magnitude and persistence of human suffering. When they lose hope, the whole thing falls apart.

Bumps in the road should not be cause for alarm. Rather, they should be the impetus for greater action. Resilient working relationships can weather upset to a point. However, everything has its breaking point. If a downturn in continuity serves as a harbinger of the decay of other elements of the work relationship, that's when you're actually in trouble.

Four rings to rule them all

Thought leadership, mission statements, and company values are full of attributes to describe why and how we work: passion, collaboration, determination, grit, drive, a servant's heart, respect, loyalty, family, care, dedication, calling, accountability, ownership, stewardship, etc. Having taken a close look at continuity, reciprocity, purpose, and hope, and having seen their interplay in action, it would

---

[26] See Redfield, P. (2013). Life in Crisis: The Ethical Journey of Doctors Without Borders. University of California Press.

be more than fair at this point to wonder why these four only? Why these four specifically?

Continuity, reciprocity, purpose, and hope are the aspects of our working relationships that are most consistently within our locus of control, both as individuals and as leaders. These are the things we can most readily sustain without outside influence, with just our internal locus of control. Passion, so commonly cited in mission statements and interviews as a requirement for being a good fit in company culture, is fleeting by nature. Despite what cooking competition shows like to say, you can't make yourself passionate about something any more than you can force yourself to believe in Santa again. Hope, on the other hand, can be cultivated.

These four elements are also distinguished by the object they aim to produce. Collaboration, for example, is similar to reciprocity in that it requires the input of two parties. However, the product of collaboration is a piece of work—a product or a service. If there isn't a thing to be produced, collaboration isn't really necessary. Reciprocity aims to create a relationship. The point is not a product, although those benefit from a reciprocal relationship, but rather the working relationships that make collaborative work possible in the first place. This isn't to say that collaboration isn't important—it's vital to working well. Yet reciprocity, like continuity, purpose, and hope, is more primal. The absence of collaboration is only felt in moments of production. The absence of reciprocity is felt all the time, a fundamental hole in the human connections that inspire and sustain working lives.

Further, these elements are interconnected. In encountering one of these elements, the others so often manifest as well. There is something innately interconnected about these aspects of our working selves. Anthropologists look for patterns within and across the places and cultures we study. If something happens repeatedly, especially across different contexts, that's a sure sign that that something is significant. Continuity, reciprocity, purpose, and hope consistently appear *together* across industries, continents, and field sites. I believe this is because, while the kinds of work we do varies incredibly from place to place and time to time, the relationships that underwrite that work, and what humans want from those relationships, remain consistent. Ideas like grit and ownership may be momentarily fashionable to describe the work we do, but continuity, reciprocity, purpose, and hope describe who humans are as working *creatures*.

And because these elements are closest to describing the nature of who humans are and why they do what they do (at least in the context of work), they also have the greatest influence on what allows us to maintain that essential nature: resilience. *We work to live*. Resilience is our fundamental capacity to keep working, and keep living, come what may. Without resilience, we're undone. The game cannot persist. The only thing that is certain in the world of work is change. The only thing we can truly control is our ability and capacity to meet and absorb that change. Continuity, reciprocity, purpose, and hope are the elements of our working relationships that best enable us to cultivate resilience, and the prime suspects when our resilience falters.

ASK IT YOURSELF

"People will be wondering what the hell to do with this. Any clarity is helpful." - Steve Smith

Rather than a traditional "here's what I talked about" conclusion, I thought I would end with something more fitting to the practical theme of this book. If you've read this far and agree with some of the ideas, but are unsure of how to take the next steps as either an individual or a leader, I've put together this field guide to start you on your way. As I noted in the introduction, this section is not a step-by-step guide on how to unlock working relationships in your organization or maximize your self-actualization. This isn't a *Working Relationship for Dummies*. Rather, consider this a DIY-style manual, but one that lays out a series of things to consider and questions to ask so that you can perform your own ethnographic research on yourself and, if you are so inclined, your organization.

Let's start with an inventory of what's in your control and what's not.

A shared locus of control

As I argued in an earlier chapter work is an experience of partial control. There are the aspects of work over which we have greater control—the copy we write, the ingredients we select—and there are aspects over which we have less control, like how an audience receives that advertisement or beer. Working relationships are created, maintained, advanced, and destroyed through a similar shared locus of control.

Your personal level of control will vary depending on whether you're an employee or an employer, or an individual contributor or leader. Timing, seasonality, economic conditions, moods, and a whole bunch of other things that you can't really do anything about will also influence your control. Lastly, I've found that the different elements themselves allow differing levels of control from different parties. The short answer is that it's complicated. The longer answer is that the social, personal, economic, and other contextual factors that can influence continuity, reciprocity, purpose, or hope are incredibly nuanced.

You need a practical strategy for cultivating working relationships. It doesn't do you or anyone else any good to hammer away at an aspect of a relationship that you can't effectively influence. Rather, you should focus your energy, resources, and mental/emotional capacity where you can make the greatest impact. Let's look at the elements one by one.

Continuity

Continuity is the trust that working relationships will endure. As such, continuity is a shared project. Control is determined by your position in the relationship—employee, contractor, leader, employer, etc.—and how you define an enduring relationship, be it continual employment, a steady stream of contracts, or a consistently competitive footing in an unstable job market.

As an individual, you can develop skills and collect experiences that will make you valuable to employers or clients and competitive on the job market. Building a strong understanding of the industries and markets in which you operate, as an employee or independent contractor, will help you read the weather and position yourself for the best opportunities. If your goal is to remain with a particular employer for the long haul, you can control the potential value you bring to the relationship. You cannot control whether the employer will see your skills and knowledge as valuable, and even if they do see your value, you cannot control whether they'll be willing to pay the cost of retaining that value. If your goals lie in contract employment, the same rules still apply to what you can or can't control, albeit with a defined end date for each engagement and the potential for more contracts to follow.

As a leader or employer, your control lies in how much confidence you build in your employees and contractors that their choosing you was a sound decision. Don't make promises you can't keep. It is unlikely that you will be able to promise job security from hire to retirement. So don't say your goal is that this will be the last job they ever have. Rather, focus on the promises you can keep because they are within your locus of control: engaging development opportunities, meaningful rewards and recognition, a purpose-driven environment, a career where people can hope.

Reciprocity

Reciprocity is the equivalent exchange through which we start, perpetuate, and advance working relationships. Reciprocity is the same assignment for each party: give, receive, and reciprocate. Individual contributors give their discretionary effort. Employers and contracting parties reciprocate that effort with meaningful gifts like competitive or added compensation, development opportunities, and additional contracts.

While both parties have control, reciprocal working relationships are almost always asymmetrical. Employers generally have more power in a relationship than employees, as do patrons over their contractees. This shouldn't be particularly alarming—we reconcile asymmetrical relationships in our personal lives daily—e.g., parents to children. It is important, though, to be conscious of these power differentials because they influence expectations: a child may be expected to clean their room, but they aren't expected to pay the bills. That's a parent's job. In the same way, employers should be aware of their outsized ability to impact the life of an employee compared with the employee's ability to impact them. The expectations surrounding who should give what and when should follow the same logic.

Purpose

Purpose is the belief and validation that your work is meaningful. Purpose is highly demarcated depending on your position. Simply put, finding purpose is the sole responsibility of the individual. No employer, mentor, leader, friend, or inspirational book can give you true purpose. What makes work meaningful to you is deeply personal, and your belief in whether the work you're doing activates that meaning is a matter of personal reflection.

Likewise, a leader or employer's responsibility is not to find purpose for others. Missions, visions, and values can suggest actions your people should take, but they can't assign meaning to those actions, even if they explicitly state how you're supposed to feel when you "collaborate" or "strive" or "leave it all on the field." Rather, your job is to learn about the purpose that drives individuals in your organization and do your best to validate their purpose within reasonable means. If an employee works to support their family or be the best in their field, are you setting them up the best you can to achieve that purpose?

Hope

Hope is the optimism that things can change for the better, and the will to pursue that change. Like purpose, control over hope is heavily role-based. Employers and leaders cannot make their employees hopeful. Not to sound cheesy, but hope comes from within. It's a deeply idiosyncratic practice that individuals have to learn for themselves through trial and error. Leaders can support that learning process by creating spaces that embrace change and reframe good-faith failures as growth opportunities. This is what it means to inspire hope in someone else: It's not to give them hope, but give them the means to hope.

For the individual: Me-search

A solid understanding of working relationships begins with a solid understanding of the character and quality of your own working relationships. To start taking action, whether for yourself or your organization, you need to benchmark where you stand. Answering a series of ethnographic questions can offer useful insight.

Continuity: *What would motivate you to still be in your current line of work in one year? What would discourage you? What would motivate you to still be in your current organization one year from now? What would discourage you?*

Rather than asking the tried-and-true "Where do you see yourself in five years?"—imagine what would encourage or discourage you from sticking with a company. The goal is not to envision yourself in some far-off land of "five years from now," which isn't really tangible or practical, but rather to take an inventory of what is adding to your current relationship with the work you do and the people and organization you do it with it, and what is subtracting from it. If the subtractions outnumber the additions, that's cause for concern.

Reciprocity: *When was the last time you felt truly recognized and rewarded for your contributions to this company?*

Again, a two-parter. On one hand, consider a time when you did something that ought to have been recognized and rewarded. What was the discretionary effort involved in this action? How did it make you feel? On the other, did the organization live up to your expectation for reciprocating that discretionary effort?

Purpose: *What do you find meaningful? How often are you able to pursue that meaning in your work?*

The question is not "What do you find meaningful about your work at the company?" Rather, it's "What do you find meaningful *in general?"* Think about what you find meaningful beyond work. Itemize it. Then, consider whether you are able to consistently and adequately pursue what you find meaningful through your work. If there is a disconnect between what you find meaningful and the opportunities your work presents to pursue that meaning, note that.

Hope: *In general, do you feel you're moving forward, moving backward, or not moving at all? In your career? In your life?*

Hope is the belief in positive change. This question considers your basic level of optimism concerning your career and life movement. If you're moving forward, is it where you want to go? If you feel you're moving backward, can you redirect your momentum toward some other target? If you feel like you're stuck in a rut, what can you do differently today to unstick yourself?

Now that you have an idea of where you are at, make some moves. I could write some step-by-step self-reflection and journaling cadence to advise on how best to implement these ideas. I initially drafted one out, but I scrapped it. The fact is, how you live and work with your working relationships is your journey. I can't prescribe a course of action other than that thinking through and talking about the state of your working relationships is good. If you're not thinking about your own working relationships, you're missing out on an important opportunity to connect with yourself and deepen your connection to what you do and who and what you do it with.

For the leader: Become an office ethnographer

Resilient working relationships are cultivated by the presence of continuity, reciprocity, purpose, and hope. For your overall organizational health, your scores don't need to be top-notch across the board (although that can be a worthy goal). Like an undergrad feverishly comparing grades on past assignments and exams to see if they'll be able to average out a B this semester, highs in some elements can balance out lows in another to promote overall resilient working relationships. Knowing your strengths and weaknesses, what is working well and what needs improvement, is essential to creating and maintaining a sustainable, actionable strategy for achieving the working relationships you want.

If you aren't sure where you stand, and whether your organization is actively promoting (or undermining) these elements, don't worry. It's not too late. In fact, now is exactly the time to start asking questions. Literally. Go talk to people. Schedule some one-on-ones. Send a pulse survey. Spend some time around the coffee maker just listening. Use the tools that you have and the connections you have already cultivated to do some office ethnography.

The essence of ethnography is a combination of observation and questioning designed to get people who know deeply what they know, but may not be comfortable sharing what they know, or may not even realize that other people don't know what they know, to open up. The goal is for respondents to identify those things that come without saying because they go without saying, and actually say them. The process of having to describe, either out loud or in writing, what usually goes undescribed is revealing for both the participant and the researcher.

To get you started, here is a set of ethnographic research techniques you can use to assess the working relationships in your organization. You'll notice that these questions are similar to the self-reflection questions from the me-search section. This is a tenet of ethical research: We should be willing and prepared to candidly answer the questions we ask of others if we hope to receive candid answers from them. If you are a leader engaging in office ethnography, I cannot recommend strongly enough that you should answer the previous questions yourself—and have those answers on hand during your study—before launching the following questions with your organization.

Promise benchmarking

In the past 12 months, how many promises have you made to employees, explicit or implicit? How many of those promises have you kept? How many are pending? How many have you broken?

Look through all of the communications you've sent over the past 12 months—emails, private messages, sticky notes, etc. (I know that's a pain, but trust me, it will be worth it)—and make a note of all of the promises you've made to people at your organization, be they employees, supervisors, or clients. Now consider the current status of those promises. Have you kept any? Have you broken any? Are there some you haven't made any progress on, but still plan to? Are there some that you've made some progress on? Calculate the percentages for each category: kept, pending, broken. This is your promise scorecard for the last year.

Try not to be discouraged if the percentages look bad. This is your benchmark. For the next 12 months, you can improve your promise metrics in two ways: making fewer promises you can't keep and more you can, and by working harder to fulfill the promises you have made.

Nobody is perfect. Sometimes things outside of your control will impact your ability to keep a promise. That's okay. If you consistently keep promises, breaking a promise becomes the exception, not the expectation.

Evaluate whether your organization is a good partner

If you were in your employees' position, would you describe that relationship as reciprocal by your current standards?

Don't apply what you remember your standards being back when you actually were in their position. We've all heard enough to make us jaded to "back in my day" justifications. The facts are: (1) Humans tend to idealize the past, remembering the highlights of their experience rather than the lowlights, and embellishing as distance from the experience morphs into nostalgia for it, and (2) even if those were accurate standards at that point in time, we are no longer at that point in time. Times change, and with them expectations as to what is typical, proper, and good.

Instead, apply your current standards for a healthy, productive, reciprocal relationship. The standards you have as a director of such and such or a VP of whatever. The standards you would want if you were a CEO or a founder. The standards you would expect out of a team of like-minded people.

If, upon reflection, you realize that your current standards are relatively low, then that's something to address in your own relationships.

If you feel justified in maintaining a less-than-reciprocal relationship with your employees because you feel you have a less-than-reciprocal relationship with those you report to, that sucks. It's something you should definitely address. But if you use your own shitty situation to justify what you know to be bad conditions for those who look to you for a reciprocal relationship, you might be an asshole.

Create a purpose map

If you had to name the top three things that motivate you to come to work every day, what would they be? No bullshit, no judgment. What are your real top three?

Take the opportunity in the next professional development meeting or annual review or whatever your organization does to track performance and sentiment to ask this question to each and every employee. Insist on a "top three." This shows that there can be more than one answer per individual, allowing more complex answers, but the hard limit forces them to prioritize. What is truly top of mind and soul for them? Also, insist that you want candid answers—you're not looking for them to parrot the mission statement or ramble off some company values. This is about them, what they want, and where they want to go. If you don't feel your employees will honestly share that information with you, work on being more open and transparent with them. Model the candor you hope to receive.

Once you have a running list of employee purposes, create a purpose map. Sort and group folks with similar purposes (a whiteboard or FigJam really helps with this). Compare those with aligned purposes. Those with divergent purposes. What are the firmographic, demographic, and psychographic commonalities of those with shared purposes?

Once you have a map, strategize! Consider ways to bring people with similar purposes together as a source of interpersonal support. Maybe it's a book club around a shared interest. Maybe it's skill development. Maybe it's a social club that meets outside working hours. As an employer, you have a responsibility to create an environment that validates employee purpose. However, when it comes to actually validating that purpose, you don't have to do it alone.

Design a hope index

In the past 12 months, what at your organization has changed? What were the big innovations? What were the small innovations? When was the last time someone in leadership shared a radical idea? How often do employee ideas bubble up to senior leadership meetings?

Similar to creating a promise benchmark, your goal in asking these questions is to identify whether you work in and encourage a hopeful space, a space that promotes meaningful change. Ask these questions of yourself. Ask these questions of people you trust to give you an informed, honest answer. Give your organization a score—7/10, four stars, a crocodile—it doesn't matter, just something that is meaningful to you that you can use for current analysis and future longitudinal comparison.

Compare your findings against key performance indicators or metrics your organization consistently tracks. Employee sentiment from eNPS, retention, employee referrals, win-loss analysis. Anything that gives you insight into how people feel about working with or for your organization. Overall, do employees and customers seem engaged or disengaged?

If it's the latter, you may be stagnating. Identify the biggest blockers for change and unblock them. Compare your progress at unblocking against your index score and your KPIs in three months. Did you go from a five to a six? More important, do things at your organization feel different? Better? More hopeful? Less boring or monotonous? If so, you're on the critical path.

Your own personal resilience

My "Ask It Yourself" advice up to this point has focused around how to collect and digest data about your working relationships and the working relationships of others. So what's next? That's a great question, and not one that I have a prescriptive answer for. This isn't a book to help you be a better worker or achieve a better career. It's not a how-to guide or an action plan. Rather, this book, and theory of working relationships in general, is to help you diagnose the quality of your working context, and to better understand and articulate to others why things in your work and your career are going well or are falling apart.

At the end of the introduction, I asked a personal diagnostic question:

On a scale of zero to 10, with zero being not at all and 10 being extremely, how resilient is your relationship to work?

Having read about continuity, reciprocity, purpose, and hope, and having considered the presence of each in your working relationships, I would invite you to revisit this question. Has your score changed at all? If so, why? What will you do about it?

I point out in places that you should be cautious if working relationships don't provide the elements you need. However, I'm not saying that you should or shouldn't work in places that don't have continuity, reciprocity, purpose, or hope. That's not really my place. The work of Doctors Without Borders is important, and it shouldn't cease because the job falls short on reciprocation or continuity. Rather, I think it's important for people to go into working relationships with as much understanding of what they're getting into as possible, and to keep an open dialogue with themselves about how it's going, for better or worse. Through that understanding, you'll be in a better, more strategic position to make the best next move. What that move looks like is up to you.

Prescribing a treatment for working relationships is not my purview. You should do what you want. For me to tell you what you should do or what you should not do cuts against one of the core themes of this book: that your working relationships are a deeply personal journey. I believe that you know in your heart the answer to all of these questions set forth in this book. And you know what you are capable of doing and want to do about those relationships far better than I ever could.

Again, my goal here is to present the concepts and language for you to open up a conversation about working relationships. Understanding when work *works* and when it doesn't *for us* is valuable information. If this book has encouraged you to start collecting this data, then I feel I've been successful.

The truth is, too, that you and I are in the same boat. I'm at the point where I've figured out the right questions to ask, and have begun answering them for myself. There is no how-to book to write next. My journey is my own, as is yours to you.

And while I may not know your journey (or even mine at this point), I know what the destination looks like, if vaguely. In the end, the point of all this questioning, analyzing, and storytelling around continuity, reciprocity, purpose, and hope is to inspire us to ask questions toward building resilient working relationships. Resilient relationships are continuous, reciprocal, purposeful, and hopeful. Resilient relationships can be counted on to endure. They give and take in a sustainable and mutually strengthening equilibrium. They inspire us to action and celebrate our perseverance. They have the potential to change and grow for the better. By asking ourselves and others how we approach promises, how we invest, what we find purposeful, and what we pursue with hope, we will have a fighting chance at creating relationships that can endure and thrive in a world of work that is consistently, but only partially, beyond our control.

BIBLIOGRAPHY

Acitelli, T. (2013). *The audacity of hops: The history of America's craft beer revolution.* Chicago: Chicago Review Press

Alexander, J. W. (2013). *Brewed in Japan: The evolution of the Japanese beer industry.* Vancouver, UBC Press.

Allen, M. (2002). *Identity and resistance in Okinawa.* Lanham, MD: Rowman & Littlefield Publishers.

Allison, A. (1994). *Nightwork: Sexuality, pleasure, and corporate masculinity in a Tokyo hostess club.* Chicago: University of Chicago Press.

Allison, A. (2006). *Millennial monsters: Japanese toys and the global imagination.* Berkeley, CA: University of California Press.

Allison, A. (2013). *Precarious Japan.* Durham, NC: Duke University Press.

American Psychiatric Association. (2013). *Diagnostic and statistical manual of mental disorders* (5th ed.). Arlington, VA.

Andrews, T. M. (2017, May 5). "'Treachery': Craft brewery Wicked Weed enrages fans by partnering with big beer." *Chicago Tribune.* Retrieved from https://www.chicagotribune.com/business/ct-wicked-weed-inbev-backlash-20170505-story.html

Appadurai, A. (1986). *The Social life of things: Commodities in cultural perspective.* Cambridge: Cambridge University Press.

Bennett, J. (2010). *Vibrant matter: A political ecology of things.*

Durham, NC: Duke University Press.

Bernot, K. (2015). "The past—and future—of Japanese craft beer." *Draft Magazine.*

Borovoy, A. B. (2005). *The too-good wife: Alcohol, codependency, and the politics of nurturance in postwar Japan.* Berkeley: University of California Press.

Bostwick, W. (2014). *The brewer's tale: a history of the world according to beer.* New York: W.W. Norton & Company.

Bourdain, A. (2000). *Kitchen confidential: Adventures in the culinary underbelly.* New York: Bloomsbury.

Bourdieu, P. (1977). *Outline of a theory of practice.* Cambridge, U.K: Cambridge University Press.

Bourdieu, P. (1984). *Distinction: A social critique of the judgement of taste.* Cambridge, Mass: Harvard University Press.

Brewers Association (2019, May/June). "Rankings." *The New Brewer, 36*(3), 125-200.

Brewers Association. (n.d.). *Craft beer industry market segments.* Retrieved from https://www.brewersassociation.org/statistics-and-data/craft-beer-industry-market-segments/

Brewers Association. (n.d.). *First look at new on-premise sales price data.* Retrieved from https://www.brewersassociation.org/insights/first-look-at-new-on-premise-sales-price-data/

Brewers Association. (n.d.). *State craft beer sales & production statistics, 2018.* Retrieved from https://www.brewersassociation.org/

statistics-and-data/state-craft-beer-stats/

Brodwin, P. (2013). *Everyday ethics: Voices from the front line of community psychiatry.* Berkeley: University of California Press.

Calagione, S. (2005). *Brewing up a business: Adventures in entrepreneurship from the founder of Dogfish Head Craft Brewery.* Hoboken, NJ: John Wiley.

Callon, M. (1986). "Some elements of a sociology of translation: Domestication of the scallops and the fishermen of St. Brieuc Bay," pp.196-223, in J. Law (eds.), *Power, action and belief: A new sociology of knowledge?* London, Routledge.

Chapman, N. G. (2017). *Untapped: Exploring the cultural dimensions of craft beer.* Morgantown: West Virginia University Press.

Christensen, P. A. (2015). *Japan, alcoholism, and masculinity: Suffering sobriety in Tokyo.* London: Lexington Books.

Christy, A. (1993). "The making of imperial subjects in Okinawa." *Positions: East Asia Cultures Critique.* 1:3.

Collinson, P. and H. M. Macbeth (2011). "The thirst for tradition: Beer production and consumption in the United Kingdom." pp.89-99, in W. Schiefenhövel and H. M. Macbeth (eds.), *Liquid bread: Beer and brewing in cross-cultural perspective.* New York: Berghahn Books.

Crowell, C. (2017, May 2). "Why do breweries fail? We search for the one true answer (and fail)." *Craft Brewing Business.* Retrieved from https://www.craftbrewingbusiness.com/business-marketing/why-craft-breweries-fail/

Delgaty, A. (2020). *Heart and matter: Fermentation in a time of crisis.* Doctoral dissertation, The University of North Carolina at Chapel Hill. Department of Anthropology.

Delgaty, A. (2021). "Japan's disaster artisans." *Anthropology News.* September 29, 2021.

Delgaty, A. (2023). "The lessons I learned about work relationships from my years brewing craft beer." *Fast Company.* August 17, 2023.

Delgaty, A. and E. R. Wilson. (2022). "Craft brewing's hiring crisis, and the challenges of a 'passion-driven' career." *Fast Company.* April 22, 2022.

Delgaty, A. and E. R. Wilson. (2023). "The hidden strains of 'cool' jobs." *Sociology.*

Desjarlais, R. R. (1992). *Body and emotion: The aesthetics of illness and healing in the Nepal Himalayas.* University of Pennsylvania Press.

Downey, G. (2005). *Learning capoeira: Lessons in cunning from an Afro-Brazilian art.* Oxford: Oxford University Press.

Figal, G. A. (2012). *Beachheads: War, peace, and tourism in postwar Okinawa.* Lanham, MD: Rowman & Littlefield.

Furnari, C. (2017, May 3). "Anheuser-Busch to purchase Wicked Weed Brewing." *Brewbound.* Retrieved from https://www.brewbound.com/news/anheuser-busch-purchase-wicked-weed-brewing

Furnari, C. (2018, March 27). "A record number of breweries opened in 2017, but closures are on the rise." *Brewbound.* Retrieved from https://www.brewbound.com/news/record-number-breweries-opened-2017-closures-rise

Gatza, P. (2018, December 18). "Brewers Association board updates: Craft brewer definition, taproom class, political action committee." *Brewers Association*. Retrieved from https://www.brewersassociation.org/industry-updates/brewers-association-board-updates-2018/

Gatza, P. and B. Watson. (2019). "Challenges & resilience in 2018." *The New Brewer, 36*(3), 41-46.

Glenn, A. F. (2018). *Asheville beer: An intoxicating history of mountain brewing.* Charleston, SC: The History Press.

Goffman, E. 1951. "Symbols of Class Status." *British Journal of Sociology, 2*(4) 294-304.

Graeber, D. (2011). *Debt: The first 5,000 years.* Melville House.

Graeber, D. (2018). *Bullshit jobs: A theory.* Simon & Schuster.

Gribbins, K. (2015, November 16). "What are the historic success and failure rates of breweries?" *Craft Brewing Business*. Retrieved from https://www.craftbrewingbusiness.com/business-marketing/historic-success-rates-brewing-abnormal-beer-announces-1-million-expansion-six-months-makes-us-muse/

Grossman, K. (2013). *Beyond the pale: The story of Sierra Nevada Brewing Co.* Hoboken, NJ: Wiley.

Hankins, J. D. (2014). *Working skin: Making leather, making a multicultural Japan.* Berkeley: University of California Press.

Harrison, J. (2005). "Spam." pg. 185-98. in *Fat: An anthropology of an obsession*. In Kulick, D. and A. Meneley. (eds.). Penguin Publishing. New York.

Heath, D. and A. Meneley. (2010). "The naturecultures of foie gras: Techniques of the body and a contested ethics of care." *Food, Culture and Society* 13, no. 3, pg. 421–52.

Helf, K. (2019, April 10). "Beer notes: Glitter beer sparks controversy (it's still pretty, though)." *Shore Craft Beer.* Retrieved from https://shorecraftbeer.com/beer-notes-glitter-beer-sparks-controversy-its-still-pretty-though/

Heying, C. H. (2010). *Brew to bikes: Portland's artisan economy.* Portland, OR: Ooligan Press, Portland State University.

Hindy, S. (2014). *The craft beer revolution: how a band of microbrewers is transforming the world's favorite drink.* New York, NY: St. Martin's Press.

Hindy, S. and T. Potter (2005). *Beer school: Bottling success at the Brooklyn Brewery.* Hoboken, NJ: Wiley.

Hooley, D. (2016, April 11). "'Don't be mean to people: A golden rule saison' is the official beer against HB 2." *INDY Week.* Retrieved from https://indyweek.com/food-and-drink/news/don-t-mean-people-golden-rule-saison-official-beer-hb-2/

Ingold, T. (2000). *The perception of the environment: Essays on livelihood, dwelling and skill.* London: Routledge.

Ingold, T. (2011). *Being alive: Essays on movement, knowledge and description.* London: Routledge.

"Is marijuana legalization a threat to craft beer?" (2016, November). *American Craft Beer.* Retrieved from https://www.americancraftbeer. com/marijuana-legalization-threat-craf

Jay, B. (2013, November 25). "Yo-Ho brewing: A window into craft beer in Japan." *Serious Eats.*

Kawano, S. (2010). *Nature's embrace: Japan's aging urbanites and new death rites.* Honolulu: University of Hawai'i Press.

Keating, K. (2023). *The trusted learning advisor: The tools, techniques, and skills you need to make L&D a business priority.* Kogan Page.

Kell, J. (2017, May 3). "Anheuser-Busch InBev just bought its 10th craft brewer." *Fortune.* Retrieved from http://fortune. com/2017/05/03/abinbev-tenth-craft-brewer-deal/

Klein, S. (2011, August 1). "Bottoms up, litigation down: Microbrewers forsake litigation, opt for collaborative blend." *ABA Journal.* Retrieved from http://www.abajournal.com/magazine/ article/bottoms_up_litigation_down_microbrewers_forsake_ litigation_opt_for_collabor

Knight, J. (1994). "Rural revitalization in Japan: Spirit of the village and taste of the country." *Asian Survey 34, no. 7,* pg. 634-646.

Knoedelseder, W. (2012). *Bitter brew: the rise and fall of Anheuser-Busch and America's kings of beer.* New York: Harper Business.

Kondo, D. K. (1990). *Crafting selves: Power, gender, and discourses of identity in a Japanese workplace.* Chicago, IL: The University of Chicago Press.

Latour, B. (1988). *The pasteurization of France*. Cambridge, MA: Harvard University Press.

Latour, B. (2005). *Reassembling the social: An introduction to actor-network-theory*. Oxford: Oxford University Press.

Lévi-Strauss, C. (1966). *The savage mind*. Chicago, Il. The University of Chicago Press.

Loftus, W. R. (1874). *The brewer: A familiar treatise on the art of brewing, with directions for the selection of malt and hops. Instructions for making cider and British wines. Also, a description of the new and improved brewing saccharometer and slide rule ...* London: W. R. Loftus.

Malinowski, B. (1984). *Argonauts of the western Pacific: An account of native enterprise and adventure in the archipelagoes of Melanesian New Guinea*. Prospect Heights, Ill: Waveland Press.

Marx, Karl. 1978 [1867] "Capital, Volume One, Chapter 1: Commodities" in *The Marx-Engel Reader*, Second Edition. New York: W.W. Norton & Company. Pp. 302-329.

Mauss, M. (1967). *The gift: Forms and functions of exchange in archaic societies*. New York: Norton.

McCarthy, N. (2016, November 1). "Which U.S. cities have the most microbreweries per capita?" *Forbes*. Retrieved from https://www.forbes.com/sites/niallmccarthy/2016/11/01/which-u-s-cities-have-the-most-microbreweries-per-capita-infographic/#32b74055e19b

McGovern, P. E. (2017). *Ancient brews: Rediscovered and recreated*. New York: W.W. Norton & Company.

Meigs, A. (1997). "Food as a cultural construction." pg. 95-106, *In Food and Culture: A Reader.* Edited by Carole Counihan and Penny Van Esterik. Routledge.

Meli, M. (2013). *Craft beer in Japan: The essential guide.* Yokohama, Japan: Bright Wave Media.

Meneley, A. (2004). "Extra virgin olive oil and slow food." *Anthropologica*, 46(2), 165-176.

Mol, A. (1999). "Ontological politics: A word and some questions." In J. Law and J. Hassard, eds. *Actor-Network Theory and After*. Pp. 74-89. Oxford: Blackwell.

Morales, D. (2016). "Beer essentials: The craft beer boom in Japan shows no sign of running dry." *The Japan Times*. Retrieved from https://www.japantimes.co.jp/life/2016/06/04/food/beer-essentials-craft-beer-boom-japan-shows-no-sign-running-dry/#. XcMnX0VKh24

Moretti, E. (2012). *The new geography of jobs*. New York: Houghton Mifflin Harcourt.

Mull, A. (2019, April 2). "Millennials are sick of drinking, but they're not giving up booze just yet." *The Atlantic*. Retrieved from https://www.theatlantic.com/health/archive/2019/04/millennials-sober-sick-of-drinking/586186/

Murphy, B. (2014). *Brewing identities: Globalisation, Guinness and the production of Irishness*. New York: Peter Lang.

Myers, E. L. and S. H. Ficke (2016). *North Carolina craft beer and breweries (2nd ed.)*. Winston-Salem, NC: John F. Blair Publishing.

Nagata, M. L. (2007). "Apprentices, servants, and other workers: Apprenticeship in Japan," pp. 35-45, in Munck, B. D., Kaplan, S. L., & Soly, H. (eds.), *Learning on the shop floor: Historical perspectives on apprenticeship*. New York: Berghahn Books.

日本ビアジャーナリスト協会 (Japan Beer Journalist Association, eds.) (2015). 日本のクラフトビール図鑑 *(Japan craft beer field guide)*. 東京, 日本. 株式会社マイナビ.

Noel, J. (2018). *Barrel-aged stout and selling out: Goose Island, Anheuser-Busch, and how craft beer became big business.* Chicago: Chicago Review Press.

Nordstrom, C. (2004). *Shadows of war: Violence, power, and international profiteering in the twenty-first century.* Berkeley: University of California Press.

Ocejo, R. E. (2017). *Masters of craft: Old jobs in the new urban economy.* Princeton, NJ: Princeton University Press.

Ogden, L. (2011). *Swamplife: People, gators, and mangroves entangled in the Everglades.* Minneapolis: University of Minnesota Press.

Oliver, G. (2012). *The Oxford companion to beer.* New York: Oxford University Press.

Papazian, C. (2003). *The complete joys of homebrewing, 3rd edition.* New York: Harper Collins.

Paxson, H. (2013). *The life of cheese: Crafting food and value in America.* Berkeley: University of California Press.

Peters, B. (2018, May 29). "Will marijuana industry overtake beer as legalization spurs innovation?" *Investor's Business Daily.* Retrieved from https://www.investors.com/news/marijuana-industry-cannabis-business-threaten-beer-industry-420/

Rao, S. (2019). "Baltimore brewers clap back at review culture with '2 Stars Not My Style' sour." *Baltimore Sun.* Retrieved from https://www.baltimoresun.com/food-drink/bs-fo-two-stars-not-my-style-20191007-20191007-6rlfdt5udjempj7pys2ld4hqyq-story.html

Redfield, P. (2013). *Life in crisis: The ethical journey of Doctors Without Borders.* Berkeley: University of California Press.

Reinarz, J. (2007). "Learning by brewing: Apprenticeship and the English brewing industry in the late Victorian and early Edwardian period," pp. 111-132, in Munck, B. D., Kaplan, S. L., & Soly, H. (eds.), *Learning on the shop floor: Historical perspectives on apprenticeship.* New York: Berghahn Books.

Robertson, L. (2017, November 8). "Where's your head at? A look at mental health in the beer industry." *Critical Drinking, Good Beer Hunting.* Retrieved from https://www.goodbeerhunting.com/blog/2017/11/6/wheres-your-head-at-a-look-at-mental-health-in-the-beer-industry

Rogers, A. (2014). *Proof: The science of booze.* Boston: Houghton Mifflin Harcourt.

Sanders, L. J. (2023). *Empathy is not a weakness: And other stories from the edge.* Publish Your Purpose.

Shikes, J. (2017, May 4). "Craft beer bars cutting off Wicked Weed, other AB InBev-owned breweries." *Westword.* Retrieved from https://www.westword.com/restaurants/craft-beer-bars-cutting-off-wicked-weed-other-ab-inbev-owned-breweries-9033019

Sisson, P. (2015, August 5). "A Japanese brewery's zero-waste philosophy goes beyond not wasting beer." *Curbed*. Retrieved from https://www.curbed.com/2015/8/6/9933072/japanese-ecoconscious-brewery

Sparhawk, A. (2019, April 1). "BA names glitter beer 'official' competition beer style." *Craftbeer.com*. Retrieved from https://www.craftbeer.com/editors-picks/ba-names-glitter-beer-official-competition-beer-style

Solt, G. (2014). *The untold history of Ramen: How political crisis in Japan spawned a global food craze*. Berkeley: University of California Press.

Starr, B. (2023). *A humble guide to fixing everything in brand, marketing, and sales*. The Starr Conspiracy.

Traphagan, J. W. (2004). *The practice of concern: Ritual, well-being, and aging in rural Japan*. Durham, NC: Carolina Academic Press.

Traphagan, J. W. (2018). "Empty houses, abandoned graves: Negative population growth and new ideas in neo-rural Japan." *Brown Journal of World Affairs* 24, no. 2, pg. 161-174.

Walley, C. J. (2013). *Exit zero: Family and class in postindustrial Chicago*. Chicago: The University of Chicago Press.

Watson, J. L. (1997). *Golden arches east: McDonald's in East Asia*. Stanford, CA: Stanford University Press.

Weiss, B. (2016). *Real pigs: Shifting values in the field of local pork*. North Carolina: Duke University Press.

Wilgus, J. (2019). "An ongoing evolution: 25 years of craft beer in Japan." *The Japan Times*. Retrieved from https://www.japantimes.co.jp/life/2019/08/31/food/ongoing-evolution-25-years-craft-beer-japan/

Made in the USA
Middletown, DE
17 September 2024